Predicting 36-Month Attrition in the U.S. Military

A Comparison Across Service Branches

JAMES V. MARRONE

Approved for public release; distribution unlimited

RAND NATIONAL DEFENSE RESEARCH INSTITUTE

For more information on this publication, visit www.rand.org/t/RR4258

Library of Congress Cataloging-in-Publication Data is available for this publication.
ISBN: 978-1-9774-0412-1

Published by the RAND Corporation, Santa Monica, Calif.
© Copyright 2020 RAND Corporation
RAND® is a registered trademark.

Cover design by Rick Penn-Kraus
Cover images: soldier, MivPiv/Getty Images/iStockphoto; calendar, Ra/Getty Images.

Support RAND
Make a tax-deductible charitable contribution at
www.rand.org/giving/contribute

www.rand.org

Preface

Attrition during the first term of service imposes large costs on all military service branches. Past research has shown that attrition is strongly associated with several characteristics of recruits that are observable at the time of recruitment, or at least by the time of accession. Comparison across studies is difficult because different studies focus on different services, use different sets of variables, or use samples from different time periods. This study provides a comparative analysis of the predictors of attrition, using administrative data for all accessions across four service branches in fiscal years 2002 through 2013.

The analysis shows who accesses, who attrites, when they attrite, and what observable characteristics are associated with attrition at various points during the first 36 months of service. The analysis also documents the predictive power of the data to distinguish attriters from nonattriters to assess the value of recruitment and accession data in developing policies to mitigate attrition. To highlight promising avenues for future research, the author hypothesizes potential mechanisms behind attrition based on observed similarities and differences across services and over the course of the first term.

This research should be of interest to decisionmakers responsible for recruiting and retention policies, as well as scholars who study military manpower and personnel issues.

This research was sponsored by the Office of the Secretary of Defense and conducted within the Forces and Resources Policy Center of the RAND Corporation's National Defense Research Institute, a federally funded research and development center sponsored by the

Office of the Secretary of Defense, the Joint Staff, the Unified Combatant Commands, the Navy, the Marine Corps, the defense agencies, and the defense Intelligence Community.

For more information on the RAND Forces and Resources Policy Center, see www.rand.org/nsrd/ndri/centers/frp or contact the director (contact information is provided on the webpage).

Contents

Figures

Tables

Summary

First-term attrition—in which a new enlisted recruit does not complete his or her first contract—is a costly and ongoing issue across all military service branches, averaging to thousands of dollars per enlistment and millions of total dollars per year. Ensuring force readiness requires the ability to identify recruits who are of sufficiently high quality and who will also fulfill the requirements of their first term of service. Previous studies have identified several factors correlated with attrition at different points throughout the first term. The author builds on past research to conduct a cross-service comparison of whether attriters can actually be distinguished from nonattriters at the time of accession. The results provide evidence of whether attrition can be mitigated *ex-ante* by screening for various types of candidates prior to signing a contract, or whether attrition is unpredictable in advance and, therefore, requires future research to elucidate its mechanism. The report is meant to be exploratory, providing a fresh view of recent attrition patterns and generating testable hypotheses and directions for future research.

The analysis relies on data consisting of all enlisted accessions between fiscal years 2002 and 2013 in the Army, Air Force, Marine Corps, and Navy, for a total of 2,189,024 accessions from 2,034,045 unique individuals. These accession data are linked to local unemployment data from a recruit's home county. The analysis then focuses on six distinct groups of variables, according to the order in which they are observed by a recruiter: (1) geographic location and unemployment rate; (2) institutional goals, such as recruitment quotas and geopolitical climate (proxied by the year of enlistment); (3) demographic characteristics; (4) test scores and background check results; (5) medical screening results; and (6) characteristics of the contract that are somewhat at the discretion of the recruiter. The outcomes of interest are whether each accession resulted in attrition at or before various significant benchmarks during the first term: three months, six months, 12 months, and 36 months.

Three basic analyses are performed. First, the services' average recruit characteristics and attrition patterns are compared. The Army has the highest overall attrition rate, and the Marine Corps has the lowest. For all services, the attrition rate is highest prior to month 6 and levels out by month 7, staying roughly constant after that. By the end of 36 months, total attrition varies from 18.5 percent in the Marine Corps to 29.7 percent in the Army.

Next, probit regressions were used to predict the probability that a given recruit will attrite, using the sensitivity and specificity of these predictions to inform their usefulness. These are calculated as follows. The sensitivity is equal to the fraction of true attriters who are predicted correctly, and the specificity is equal to the fraction of true nonattriters who are predicted correctly. The better the regression variables are able to distinguish both attriters and nonattriters, the closer the sensitivity and specificity are to 100 percent. The results show that the full set of variables attain both sensitivity and specificity of around 60 percent for 36-month attrition, for all four services. The regressions can do only slightly better in predicting three- to 12-month attrition.

Finally, the author analyzes the marginal effect on attrition of different characteristics: gender, high school noncompleters, GED (General Educational Development, a high school diploma equivalent) holders, recruits with Entrance National Agency Check (ENTNAC, or background check) waivers, married recruits, and recruits who did not go through Delayed Entry Program (DEP). These variables were chosen because they have been found in previous research to be significantly correlated with attrition or because their patterns highlight questions for future research. The marginal effects of these characteristics show patterns that vary across services and over the course of the first term. For both types of patterns, future research can shed light on the particular mechanisms behind these attrition patterns to better suggest how to effectively mitigate attrition.

In terms of differences across services, women are more likely to attrite in the Army than in the other three services; those without a high school diploma or equivalent are most likely to attrite in the Navy. These differences highlight the potential importance of institution-specific characteristics, implying that personal characteristics may interact with institutional policy, peer groups, duties, or other aspects of military life and induce different rates of attrition in different services.

As evidenced by differences over the first term, recruits with ENTNAC waivers are no more likely than others to attrite during the first six months but are more likely to attrite after that time. (The ENTNAC consists of a check of various government agencies for evidence of an individual's suitability to enter the service.) Married recruits are more likely to attrite during the first 12 months, but those who make it past that point are less likely than other recruits to attrite later. These patterns show that different recruits have different risk periods for attrition, implying that personal characteristics may interact with individual experiences to produce different rates of attrition at different points during the first term.

Based on these results, it is unlikely that simple policies aimed at screening candidates based on their probability of attrition will be cost-effective. This is because, based on the specificities found in this analysis, predictive algorithms will screen out too many nonattriters. A large amount of attrition and nonattrition is unpredictable based on readily observable characteristics that are regularly recorded by the service branches by the time a recruit shows up to basic training. This suggests that a major cause of attrition relates to factors that are either unobservable (or, at least, not currently recorded during the enlistment process) or occur after accession. These factors might be called *fit* or a *taste* for military life, and they could relate to the service as a whole, to a particular occupation, or to a particular unit. The point is that much information is revealed *ex-post*, and research findings must link these pathways to the characteristics that can be observed during recruitment.

It is possible, however, that characteristics at accession can usefully inform retention policies in other ways. Based on what is known at accession, it may not be possible to predict with a high level of confidence that a given recruit will attrite, but it could be possible to predict their highest-risk period. The extent to which these sorts of predictions are feasible or useful will require more research: on how the services differ in first-term policies and expectations and how those differences contribute to attrition rates; on how individual recruits' pathways through the first term depend on their characteristics at accession and how those characteristics, in turn, inform how they respond to their experiences; and on whether additional information that is currently unavailable at accession—such as personality traits or noncognitive skills—may be useful in better predicting attrition.

Acknowledgments

First and foremost, thanks to Jim Hosek and particularly Beth Asch at the RAND Corporation for supervising and supporting every phase of this project. Thanks also to John Winkler and Lisa Harrington for helping initiate this research and encourage its eventual publication. Tina Panis provided programming support and valuable advice regarding the data. The author also thanks two reviewers who greatly improved the report: Michael Mattock at RAND and Lauren Malone at the Center for Naval Analysis.

Abbreviations

AFQT	Armed Forces Qualification Test
ASVAB	Armed Services Vocational Aptitude Battery
BLS	Bureau of Labor Statistics
BMI	body mass index
COMINT	Communications Intelligence
DEP	Delayed Entry Program
DMDC	Defense Manpower Data Center
DoD	U.S. Department of Defense
ENTNAC	Entrance National Agency Check
FY	fiscal year
GED	General Educational Development
PULHES	Physical capacity, Upper extremities, Lower extremities, Hearing, Eyes, and Psychiatric

CHAPTER ONE

Introduction

Background

First-term attrition is a costly phenomenon affecting all service branches. When a new enlisted soldier, airman, or sailor fails to complete the initial active-duty service contract, the service incurs a cost in the form of lost investment on that recruit, as well as the need to invest a similar amount in recruiting a replacement. In 2005, the cost per enlistment ranged from $11,000 in the Marine Corps to nearly $20,000 in the Army (roughly $14,200 to $25,800 in 2019 terms) (Dertouzos, 2009).[1] The total sunk costs due to attrition include additional outlays for training, wages, and other benefits given to recruits who leave early in their first term. In FY 2008, all of these costs were estimated at $209 million to $220 million for the Navy ($245 million to $258 million in 2019 terms) and $425 million to $479 million for the Army ($499 million to $562 million in 2019 terms) (Enns, 2012). It is, therefore, important to every service to be able to identify and recruit individuals who are most likely to serve the entirety of their first term while also being of sufficiently high quality to ensure the readiness of an all-volunteer force.

As described at length below, a large volume of recent attrition research attests to the importance of mitigating first-term attrition as part of the military's recruitment and retention goals. Collectively,

---

[1] Here and elsewhere, inflation adjustments were calculated using the Consumer Price Index at the end of the relevant fiscal year (FY), available at the St. Louis Federal Reserve FRED Database (Federal Reserve Bank of St. Louis, 2019).

these studies have identified factors correlated with attrition at different points throughout the first term. The general consensus is that certain observable variables are relatively strongly associated with attrition during the first term. For example, a recruit's sex, education, Armed Forces Qualification Test (AFQT) score, and marital status are consistently found to be statistically important predictors of attrition.

This study builds on past research to determine the degree to which various observable characteristics of recruits actually distinguish those who attrite from those who do not. In other words, the analysis focuses on variables that are known to have a strong *statistical* association with attrition to determine the degree to which they distinguish attriters *in practice*. The basic analytic approach implements the same regression analyses used by previous studies, but instead of focusing on individual variables' association with attrition outcomes, it focuses on the ability of groups of variables to explain aggregate attrition and to separately predict attriters and nonattriters. Such an analysis is a useful supplement to existing studies of attrition because it indicates the degree to which differences between attriters and nonattriters are due to observable characteristics at the time of accession—in which case, attrition could partly be mitigated through recruitment policy—or due to unobserved differences that may be more difficult to control for, including, perhaps, differences in recruits' experiences after accession.

An additional contribution of this research is the comparison of recruitment and attrition across four services using more-recent data than comparable studies. Most prior work has focused on one service. By comparing patterns across services, this analysis shows ways in which the services differ in terms of who they recruit, who attrites, and at what point during their contract they attrite. The analysis also provides evidence for which aspects of attrition are common to all branches—and therefore perhaps due to secular factors in the wider economy or to military-wide policies—versus which are unique to a given branch and therefore a function of policies unique to that service or to the pool of individuals from which that service draws recruits.

Past Literature

Attrition has long been a concern of all of the armed forces and, therefore, of researchers supporting the services' missions. In the 1960s, researchers began to evaluate the association between observable characteristics of recruits and specific benchmark outcomes, such as two- or four-year attrition in specific service branches (Plag and Hardacre, 1964; Hutchins and Kennedy, 1965; Plag and Goffman, 1966). Since then, the literature has grown to examine all service branches and has focused on several factors that appear to be strongly associated with attrition. In a review of the literature prior to 2004, Knapik et al. (2004) find that important demographic characteristics include age (attrition is highest for those 18 and under, and also high for those over age 24); gender (attrition is higher for women); and race (attrition is lower for nonwhite recruits). Attrition is also associated with lower AFQT scores, with enlistment waivers, with shorter time in the Delayed Entry Program (DEP), and with a history of felony arrests or unstable job history. In terms of physical and mental health, attrition is associated with a history of depression or physical abuse, with having a medical waiver, and with high body mass index (BMI).

Since 2004, studies have generally reaffirmed the results summarized by Knapik et al. (2004).[2] Two exceptions are Malone and Carey (2011) and Malone (2014), which find that recruits with waivers do not pose a greater attrition risk and may in fact be less likely to attrite than nonwaivered recruits; the exact combination of waivers that is most associated with attrition varies by service. These two studies also provide valuable insight into the power of accession waivers in predicting

---

[2]   Recent studies span the military services as well as attrition at different points (during DEP, training, and post-training). For analyses across all services, see Asch and Heaton (2010) and Lundquist, Pager, and Strader (2018). For the Army: Strickland (2005), Cunha et al. (2015), and Orvis et al. (2018). For the Navy: Lucas et al. (2008), Arkes and Mehay (2013), and Arkes and Cunha (2014). For the Marine Corps: Wolfe et al. (2005), Reis et al. (2007), Pollack et al. (2009), Desrosiers and Bradley (2015), and White et al. (2016).

Studies of foreign militaries have also become common in recent years and provide a comparison with U.S. attrition patterns (Kiernan, 2011; Godlewski and Kline, 2012; Hoglin and Barton, 2013).

attrition and complement the analyses here because waiver data were not available for use in this report.

Additionally, more-recent studies have begun analyzing the importance of variables characterizing recruits' experiences rather than the recruits themselves (e.g., Helmus et al., 2018). In a study of Army attrition, Buddin (2005) affirms the patterns in demographic characteristics found by prior research but also finds that the recruiting environment has large effects on DEP attrition, while the particular location of basic training is strongly associated with attrition in the first six months. More recently, Orvis et al. (2018) modeled the same outcomes as Buddin and complicated the story regarding DEP, agreeing that length of DEP is correlated with DEP attrition but also finding that it is inversely correlated with attrition (assuming the recruit gets through DEP and shows up at training).

All studies include observable characteristics of recruits and look primarily at associations and correlations—that is, they are not estimating the causal effect of certain characteristics on attrition. Thus, any policy recommendation from such evidence must be considered in context. For example, the observation that individuals from a certain group attrite at higher rates should not necessarily imply that the military enlist fewer people from that group. More information would be needed about why they attrite at greater rates—is it due to lower ability to perform their mission? Or is it due to different experiences, including actual or perceived lack of support as a soldier, airman, marine, or sailor? In favor of the latter point, Karaca-Mandic, Maestas, and Power (2013) find that women's and minorities' promotion times positively benefit from more women and minorities in leadership roles. There is currently no analogous study on attrition, although a similar relationship could hold. For example, service members who overcame particular hurdles during their first term could serve as role models for others. This research discusses several characteristics that are correlated with attrition and could indicate the presence of hurdles to success, such as being married or lacking a high school diploma.

This analysis, like the prior studies cited above, is descriptive. It does not attempt to determine optimal policies for mitigating attrition. It does, however, fill a gap in recent research by comparing accessions and attrition across four services and by examining the predictive power of observable characteristics in distinguishing attriters from nonattriters.

Approach

This research uses longitudinal data from the Defense Manpower Data Center (DMDC) covering all accessions in the Army, Air Force, Navy, and Marine Corps between FYs 2002 and 2013. This period covers the era of the Global War on Terror, up to the latest date available for analysis that still provided 36 months of observations for each recruit.[3] The data record a variety of information, including demographic characteristics, recruitment test scores, medical screening outcomes, characteristics of the enlistment contract, and local economic indicators. As discussed in more detail in Chapter Two, the precise length of the first active-duty contract and the precise reasons for leaving active-duty service cannot be identified. Therefore, the outcomes examined are three-, six-, 12-, and 36-month attrition, as well as attrition after six months, from month 7 through month 36. Attrition occurs when the individual leaves active duty for any reason. While 36-month attrition is not identical to first-term attrition (many first-term contracts are longer than three years, and some Army contracts are shorter than three years), it is a salient benchmark for all services and has been used in previous studies.[4] The analysis also considers attrition between seven and 36 months; that is, attrition conditional on serving at least six

---

[3]   For this analysis, data were available through March 2017.

[4]   Although contract length cannot be identified in the data, two-year contracts make up a small fraction of enlistments. During the period being studied, the Army offered a few two-year contracts for specific hard-to-fill occupations. For example, Buddin (2005) found that 3 percent of recruits had a two-year contract. If enlistees with two-year contracts leave between 24 and 36 months of service, they will be misclassified as 36-month attriters in this analysis. Two-year contracts, however, do not affect the calculations of attrition at the 12-month or shorter window.

months, when many recruits have completed training and are assigned to their first permanent station.[5]

The analysis proceeds in three steps. First, a summary of the data provides a cross-service comparison of who accesses and how attrition accrues over the first 36 months. This summary highlights differences between services in terms of the typical recruit profile, how many will end up attriting, and the point in their first contract at which they attrite. Next, probit regressions are estimated to assess how well different sets of variables predict attrition at different points in time. Unlike most prior studies, which look at probit regression coefficients for each individual variable, the analysis here considers the sensitivity and specificity of the overall probit model—that is, the fraction of attriters who are predicted to attrite and the fraction of nonattriters who are predicted to remain in active service. (The regression coefficients are presented in Appendix A.) The higher the sensitivity and specificity, the better the regression variables are able to collectively distinguish attriters from nonattriters. Finally, the analysis looks at the marginal effect of various characteristics over the first 36 months. In other words, what is the predicted difference in attrition rates between two groups, holding all other observable characteristics constant? This analysis shows whether attrition's association with various variables varies over the first 36 months of service, and therefore whether retention policies might be tailored to different groups of recruits early versus later in the term. To address concerns that the results may change depending on the time period studied, Appendix B provides robustness checks for the main results, limiting the sample to accessions since FY 2003 and, separately, since FY 2008.

---

[5] Although the timing of assignment to first permanent station will vary with a recruit's occupation and service branch, a six-month cutoff is appropriate to examine because in all four services, the attrition rate tapers off after this time. See Figure 2.2 and associated discussion.

CHAPTER TWO

Data Overview and Descriptive Statistics

Variables Used for Analyzing Attrition

The DMDC provided data on military accessions in FYs 2002 through 2013. The cutoff date of 2013 was chosen to ensure that the first 36 months of each recruit's term of service were observable in the data, which were available through March 2017. Each accession was observed until the individual left active duty, or 36 months, whichever came first. The data consist of observable variables recorded at the time of accession and were merged to unemployment data from the Bureau of Labor Statistics (BLS) to capture information about the labor market in the county where each recruit enlisted. The variables are listed in Table 2.1, grouped into categories based on the point during the enlistment process at which they are observable by the recruiter.

First, economic and geographic variables capture the differences in the local population's employment prospects and propensity to serve in the military. Individuals from areas of high versus low unemployment may enlist for different reasons and may therefore also face different incentives to fulfill their contract; the same is true for individuals from different regions of the country. Unemployment data were not available for U.S. territories, but dummy variables indicate which recruits came from each territory.

Next, dummy variables for each FY capture the institutional and geopolitical climate in which an individual accessed. A service's national recruitment goals, the overall economy, and international current events could all contribute to particular recruitment standards and willingness to enlist and fulfill the contract, which change over time. The FY dummy variables capture the overall effect of this environment.

Table 2.1
Variables Used in Attrition Analysis

Variable	Details
Geographic and economic variables	
County/year unemployment	Measured in percentage; from BLS, merged to DMDC county of record using county Federal Income Processing Standard code
U.S. Census region or U.S. territory	Dummy for each region (base category: South) and territory
FY	Dummy for each year (base category: 2002)
Demographic characteristics	
Female	Dummy variable
Race	5 categories: • White (base category) • Black • Asian • American Indian • Other
Hispanic ethnicity	Dummy variable
Age	4 categories: • Under 21 (base category) • 21–25 • 26–30 • Over 30
Education	6 categories: • Less than high school • High school diploma (base category) • General Educational Development (GED) or equivalent • Associate degree or less than bachelor's • Bachelor's degree • Postgraduate degree
Marital status	4 categories: • Divorced • Married • Single (base category) • Widowed
Number of children	Integer
Married with children	Dummy variable
U.S. citizen	Dummy variable
Prior active-duty service	Dummy variable

Table 2.1—Continued

Variable	Details
High school senior at time of contract	Dummy variable
Youth program participation	Dummy variable indicating participation in any of several programs
Aptitude and background test scores	
ASVAB	Percentile, calculated from raw scores among all other accessions in same service and same FY, for each of 11 categories
AFQT	Percentile
Unfavorable ENTNAC	Dummy variable indicating unfavorable ENTNAC result
Medical screening variables	
Abnormal color vision	Dummy indicating abnormal color vision
PULHES	Dummy for each category indicating some limitation (score of 2 or higher)
BMI	Continuous value, scaled so that median for both men and women is equal to 0. Also include BMI-squared.
Characteristics of contract and accession	
Month of accession	Dummy variable for each month (base category: June)
DEP	Dummy variable for 3-month increments (base category: 1–3 months), or zero
Paygrade at entry	Dummy variable (base category: E1)
Occupation at entry	10 categories based on DoD Occupational Codes: • Infantry/Seaman (base category) • Electronics • Communications Intelligence (COMINT) • Health • Other technicians • Administrative • Mechanical • Craftsworkers • Service/supply • Non-Occupational

SOURCE: DMDC data merged to BLS data at the county level.
NOTE: Variables are measured at accession, except for the characteristics of the contract and the high school senior status at the time of the contract. ASVAB = Armed Services Vocational Aptitude Battery; DoD = U.S. Department of Defense; ENTNAC = Entrance National Agency Check; PULHES = Physical capacity, Upper extremities, Lower extremities, Hearing, Eyes, and Psychiatric.

Individual demographic characteristics at the time of accession consist of mutually exclusive categorical variables recording an individual's sex, race, Hispanic ethnicity, education, marital status, age, citizenship, prior active-duty service, and participation in a service youth program.[1] In addition, the data record the number of children each individual had at the time of accession, as well as whether the individual was an unmarried parent. As an exception to the rule that variables are recorded at accession, the data additionally document whether each recruit was a high school senior at the time of signing their contract (i.e., they enlisted directly out of high school); the education-at-accession variable then indicates if they later received a diploma.

Test scores and background screenings inform not only the potential quality of a recruit, but also what occupations may be a good fit and what enlistment incentives to offer in the contract. The data record scores on 11 sections of the ASVAB as well as the AFQT. For this analysis, scores were translated into a percentile among all other accessions in the same service and same year. In addition, the data record whether the individual has a flag on their record according to the ENTNAC, which consists of a check of various government agencies for evidence of an individual's suitability to enter the service (DoD Instruction 1304.23, 2005). An unfavorable determination may indicate an individual is untrustworthy, has a criminal background, or has some other disqualifying characteristic. However, individuals with an unfavorable determination may still be allowed to enlist, depending on the particular circumstances.

Medical tests indicate whether an individual may be limited in performing certain duties, and whether they are fit enough overall for service. The data include dummy variables indicating a limitation in each of the PULHES battery of tests, a dummy variable indicating abnormal color vision, and a continuous variable recording BMI. BMI is one measure of whether a person is overweight or underweight and is equal to weight (in kilograms) divided by the square of height (in meters). Past studies have compared BMI to a particular cutoff indicat-

---

[1]   Service youth programs include the Junior Reserve Officer Training Corps, Civil Air Patrol cadets, and U.S. Naval Sea Cadets.

ing "overweight," but this report eschews that strategy for two reasons. First, the proper cutoff varies depending on the particular medical standard and service-specific weight program standard. Second, being severely underweight can also be a limitation to a recruit's performance and is a potentially disqualifying factor. Therefore, to account for being extremely over- or underweight, BMI was normalized by subtracting the median BMI for men or women and then additionally including the square of this normalized measure in the regressions. Individuals whose BMI is further from the median—in either direction—will have higher values of BMI-squared. This quadratic parameterization therefore allows us to determine whether being over- or underweight has an effect on attrition.

Finally, contract-specific variables record aspects of the individual's contract that may vary based on all of the variables already described. These contract-level characteristics include number of months in the DEP, paygrade at entry, and occupational category at entry. In addition, the analysis includes a dummy variable for the particular calendar month in which the contract was signed, to account for variation in unobservable characteristics in those who enlist over the course of a year.[2]

Characteristics of Accessions Across the Armed Forces

Table 2.2 shows the average characteristics of accessions in the data set. The services differ in attrition rates over the first 36 months of recruits' first terms. Services are most similar in three-month attrition rates, between roughly 5 percent and 6 percent for all services, but differences become apparent as the first term progresses. By the 36-month mark, attrition ranges from 18.5 percent in the Marine Corps to 29.7 percent in the Army.

---

[2]   Asch and Heaton (2010) also find that the particular day of the recruiting (not calendar) month can matter: Those recruits who are accepted at the end of the month are of lower quality. The present analysis could not replicate the approach used by Asch and Heaton because the precise day of the recruiting calendar month could not be determined.

Table 2.2
Average Characteristics of Accessions Across Service Branches, FYs 2001–2013

Variable	Army	Air Force	Navy	Marine Corps
Number of accessions	871,426	357,751	438,907	381,369
Attrition rates (percentage)				
3-month attrition	5.1	5.1	6.3	5.3
6-month attrition	9.9	9.0	8.5	7.7
12-month attrition	15.0	12.2	11.8	10.5
36-month attrition	29.7	23.1	23.6	18.5
Macroeconomic variables (%)				
Unemployment rate	6.91	6.88	6.80	6.97
West Census region	22.0	22.5	25.0	23.2
Midwest Census region	20.0	21.8	19.1	22.7
South Census region	44.3	43.1	42.1	38.0
Northeast Census region	12.4	12.1	13.2	15.6
U.S. territory	1.2	0.5	0.4	0.6
Foreign country	0.1	0.04	0.1	0.1
Demographics at accession				
Female (%)	16.2	21.4	19.4	7.5
White[a] (%)	71.8	75.5	64.1	82.3
Black (%)	17.4	17.4	20.0	11.0
Asian (%)	4.0	5.3	6.6	3.6
American Indian (%)	1.6	2.0	9.1	1.8
Other nonwhite (%)	6.3	2.1	5.9	2.1
Hispanic (%)	10.6	1.0	9.7	10.3
Under 21 (%)	54.3	67.4	65.8	79.8
21–25 (%)	30.7	28.5	26.8	17.6
26–30 (%)	9.7	3.8	5.8	2.4
Over 30 (%)	5.3	0.4	1.6	0.2
Less than high school (%)	2.6	0.5	0.4	1.5
High school diploma (%)	71.3	91.4	86.7	92.1
GED or equivalent (%)	14.5	0.7	4.5	4.7
Some college/associate degree (%)	5.8	4.1	4.0	1.9
B.A./4-year degree (%)	5.3	3.1	3.2	0.9

Table 2.2—Continued

Variable	Army	Air Force	Navy	Marine Corps
Postgraduate degree (%)	0.4	0.1	0.1	0.03
Single (%)	79.5	89.9	92.3	96.3
Married (%)	18.6	9.7	7.0	3.3
Divorced (%)	1.9	0.4	0.7	0.3
Widowed (%)	0.01	0.0	0.00	0.0
Mean number of children	0.23	0.05	0.02	0.05
Married with children (%)	10.9	3.5	2.8	0.9
Non-U.S. citizen (%)	3.6	1.8	4.4	3.2
Prior active-duty service (%)	10.1	1.9	1.4	1.8
High school senior at time of contract (%)	14.9	18.7	21.5	34.8
Youth program (%)	4.4	1.4	3.2	7.9
Test scores/background check[b]				
Mean AFQT percentile	56.2	66.6	64.1	60.4
Unfavorable ENTNAC (%)	14.4	4.7	7.9	8.2
Medical screening				
Abnormal color vision (%)	5.7	4.2	8.2	4.6
Physical strength limitation (%)	3.6	2.5	2.9	3.5
Upper extremity limitation (%)	0.7	0.5	0.6	0.4
Lower extremity limitation (%)	1.0	0.7	0.9	0.8
Hearing limitation (%)	1.6	0.7	1.0	1.1
Eye limitation (%)	20.7	20.3	20.9	20.0
Psychiatric limitation (%)	0.7	0.7	0.6	0.7
Mean BMI: men[c]	25.2	23.7	24.5	24.3
Mean BMI: women[d]	23.4	22.9	23.8	22.5
Contract variables: reflect process versus characteristics				
No DEP (%)	16.6	6.9	9.4	8.8
1–3 months DEP	43.5	16.0	23.9	30.6
4–6 months DEP	25.3	45.9	25.4	21.7
7–9 months DEP	9.2	21.1	23.8	18.4

Table 2.2—Continued

Variable	Army	Air Force	Navy	Marine Corps
10 or more months DEP	5.4	10.0	17.5	20.6
Paygrade E1 at entry (%)	41.0	70.1	51.8	72.7
Paygrade E2 (%)	25.8	10.1	22.3	25.7
Paygrade E3 (%)	21.2	17.7	25.2	0.2
Paygrade E4 or higher (%)	12.0	2.1	0.7	1.3
DoD occupation: Infantry/ Seaman (%)	17.7	2.1	74.2	0.3
Electronics (%)	5.8	0.1	0.2	0.1
COMINT (%)	11.3	0.5	0.1	0.1
Health (%)	7.8	0.8	0.05	0.0
Other technicians (%)	3.7	0.4	0.04	0.1
Administrative (%)	10.0	1.1	0.6	0.1
Mechanical (%)	12.1	3.2	24.6	0.1
Craftsworkers (%)	2.5	0.6	0.1	0.02
Service/supply (%)	13.4	1.9	0.2	0.1
Non-Occupational (%)	15.6	89.2	0.0	99.1

SOURCE: DMDC data merged to BLS data at the county level.

NOTE: Percentages within a category may not add up to 100 due to rounding.

[a] Individuals may be classified as more than one race.

[b] Regressions additionally include percentile scores for each ASVAB test category. Means are not reported in this table because they are roughly equal to 50 percent by construction.

[c] The median BMI for men is 24.4. For the regressions, BMI is measured relative to the respective male or female median.

[d] The median BMI for women is 23.4.

Underlying these attrition rates, there are both similarities and differences in the characteristics of recruits across services. The services are comparable in terms of the geographic distribution of recruits and in terms of medical test results. Differences are apparent in recruits' demographic characteristics and in how the services use enlistment incentives. The fraction of female recruits varies from 7.5 percent in the Marine Corps to 21.4 percent in the Air Force. The fraction of racial minority recruits varies as well, with the Navy having the highest ratio for each of the groups; Hispanic recruits are most common in the Army and Marine Corps. The Marine Corps also has the youngest enlistees, with

80 percent being under 21 years old and nearly all of them having a high school diploma (or equivalent) or less; likewise, the Marine Corps shows the highest proportion of recruits signing their contracts while still in high school (34.8 percent). (The variable recording high school senior status at the time of contract is used because those who sign during high school, rather than later, may have different amounts of commitment to the military or may be enlisting for different reasons, compared with those who sign after graduation.) Across the services, the majority of new recruits are single, with the Army having the highest proportion of married recruits, at 18.6 percent. The Army also has the highest proportion of recruits with prior active-duty service (10.1 percent), partially because, as explored further below, most reaccessions between services involve moves to the Army. Air Force recruits have the highest AFQT scores, which were calculated as percentiles with respect to the entire population taking the test. Few recruits have unfavorable ENTNAC results, but the Air Force has the lowest proportion (4.7 percent).

Once all the aptitude tests, medical screenings, background checks, and other information are collected, the service can offer a potential recruit a contract. The details of the contract depend on the particular profile of the recruit, as well as on service-specific rules and standards. Therefore, it would be expected that contract-level variables would be a function of the variables already discussed and may not add much new information regarding the propensity to attrite. Nevertheless, the services do differ in how they use contractual incentives in the recruiting process. The services are uniformly alike in that it is unusual for recruits to enter service directly without any time in DEP: Less than 20 percent of recruits do so in any service branch, with the largest fraction in the Army (16.6 percent) and the smallest fraction in the Air Force (6.9 percent). For those that do go through DEP, most have one to six months. The Army and Navy have the largest fraction of recruits entering at paygrades above E1, with roughly one-quarter as E2 and one-quarter as E3. The Air Force assigns fewer recruits to E2 but roughly 18 percent to E3, while the Marine Corps assigns roughly one-quarter to E2 and virtually no one higher than that. Only in the Army are there substantial numbers entering at paygrade E4 or higher (12.0 percent).

Occupational categories reflect services' different recruitment processes rather than their pools of recruits. The Army apparently has the most even distribution of recruits across different DoD occupational categories, while the Marine Corps and Air Force list nearly everyone as Non-Occupational. This, however, reflects the fact that the standard Marine Corps contract lists the occupation as a General Service Marine or a Basic Marine with Enlistment Guarantee, and the standard Air Force contract lists Basic Enlisted Airman. These services assign occupations later in the first term, so the occupation at accession is not useful for predicting attrition. The Navy splits nearly all recruits between infantry and mechanical occupations, which most commonly correspond to Seaman and Fireman jobs.

Patterns of Entry and Attrition over Time and Between Services

Overall, between FYs 2002 and 2013, there were 2,189,024 accessions from 2,034,045 unique individuals. Figure 2.1 shows how accessions

Figure 2.1
Accessions over Time, by Service

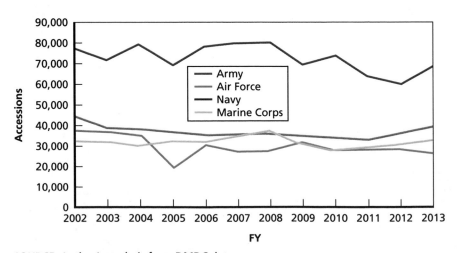

SOURCE: Author's analysis from DMDC data.

have varied over time. The Army has the most accessions, hovering between 60,000 and 80,000 each year. The other services generally have between 30,000 and 40,000 accessions each year.

Figure 2.2 shows retention through the first 36 months, for all accessions observed in the data. The figure shows the fraction of accessions for which the individual was still in active duty at given points in time during the first term. The hazard rate is highest (i.e., the line is steepest, and retention drops most quickly) over the first six months, indicating high dropout rates during training. After six to nine months, the lines are roughly straight and less steep, implying attrition occurs at a slower but roughly constant rate throughout the remaining months. The Navy and Marine Corps have the highest attrition rates during the first three months. By month six, the Army's cumulative retention rate is lower than the other services' and continues to be the lowest through the next 30 months. As noted also in Table 2.2, by month 36 the Marine Corps has the highest rate of retention, while the Army has the

Figure 2.2
Retention over the Course of the First 36 Months, by Service

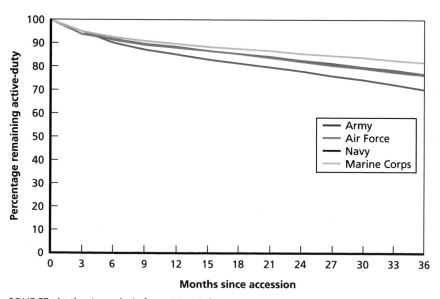

SOURCE: Author's analysis from DMDC data.

lowest, with an overall range in 36-month retention across all services, from 70.3 percent to 81.5 percent.

In the time frame studied, 99.3 percent of those individuals accessed only once; 0.7 percent (N = 15,103) accessed twice; 0.01 percent (N = 148) accessed three times, and three people accessed four times. Among those with multiple accessions, 61.8 percent reentered the same service each time. Of the 38.2 percent who did not reenter the same service, the majority (82.6 percent) moved to the Army from one of the other branches.

Those who exit and reenter generally exit early the first time but stay in service longer after the second accession. Among those with multiple observable contracts, 57 percent make it to 36 months during the first observed contract, while 76 percent make it to 36 months in the second. Among those with any prior active-duty service (including, perhaps, service before the sample observation window starts in 2001), 78 percent make it to 36 months.

CHAPTER THREE

Probit Regression Sensitivity and Specificity in Predicting Attrition

This chapter describes the predictive power of various sets of variables. The analysis uses probit regressions, a commonly used technique to analyze binary outcomes that can be characterized as a 0 (if the outcome did not occur) or 1 (if the outcome occurred). Probit regressions are the standard in the prior literature on attrition, but, unlike most prior literature, this analysis does not focus on regression coefficients for each variable individually. Rather, it examines the overall ability of the regression models to distinguish attriters from nonattriters.

To characterize the predictive power of a given regression model, the sensitivity and specificity of the model are calculated as follows. Using the coefficients from the regression, a predicted probability of attriting can be calculated for each individual. When that predicted probability is greater than or equal to the empirical probability observed in the population, that individual is assigned a predicted outcome value of 1—i.e., they are a predicted attriter. If the predicted probability is lower than the observed probability in the population, the outcome is predicted to be 0—i.e., they are predicted to continue in active duty.

Sensitivity refers to the fraction of attriters who are correctly predicted to attrite.[1] *Specificity* refers to the fraction of nonattriters who are

---

[1] To use a conceptual analogy from the medical literature, this is called the *true positive rate* and would refer to the fraction of sick people who are correctly diagnosed by a test. In the jargon of statistics, sensitivity is inversely related to the Type II error rate.

correctly predicted to stay in service.[2] If a particular set of regressors is perfectly able to predict who attrites and who does not, then the sensitivity and specificity would both be equal to 1. In general, however, there is a trade-off between the two, so that high sensitivity tends to imply low specificity.[3]

Formal Framework

To provide a conceptual example, consider first a more formal representation of the probit regression framework. For each accession, the outcome variable y_i indicates whether the accession ended in attrition by a certain time ($y_i = 1$) or not ($y_i = 0$). The probit regression models this outcome as a function of observable variables x_i, which, in this case, will be different categories of variables described in Table 2.1. The regression equation is as follows:

$$y_i = \beta'x_i + u_i \, .$$

The observable variables x_i form a $1(k + 1)$ vector (including a constant), while the regression coefficients β form a $(k + 1)1$ vector. Because the outcome variable y_i takes on only two values, the probit regression adopts a nonlinear transformation to predict values between 0 and 1 based on inputs x_i that potentially take any value. In other words, from the estimated vector of regression coefficients $\hat{\beta}$, the predicted outcome for each individual is as follows:

$$\hat{y}_i^* = \Phi(\hat{\beta}'x_i) \, .$$

The function $\Phi(\cdot)$ is the cumulative normal distribution, which takes any negative or positive input and yields a number between 0

---

[2]   This is the *true negative rate* and is inversely related to the Type I error rate.

[3]   This trade-off results from the lack of perfectly deterministic predictors that are "if and only if" markers of an outcome. Without deterministic predictors, at some point higher sensitivity must come at the expense of lower specificity. There will always be some false negatives unless every single individual is assumed to be a positive, making the specificity zero.

and 1. Thus, the predicted value $\hat{y}_i^*$ can be interpreted as the predicted probability that an individual attrites.

To compare with the observed outcome y_i, the probability $\hat{y}_i^*$ must be converted to a value of 0 or 1, which would be the predicted observed value $\hat{y}_i$. The overall population has an average attrition rate of $\bar{y}$. Comparing each predicted probability with this average, when $\hat{y}_i^* \geq \bar{y}$ the individual is predicted to attrite, so $\hat{y}_i = 1$. When $\hat{y}_i^* < \bar{y}$ the individual is predicted to stay in service, so $\hat{y}_i = 0$. Comparing the predicted and actual values allows us to classify every accession into one of four mutually exclusive groups based on the respective values of y_i and $\hat{y}_i$. For a more concrete example, consider 36-month attrition in the Army, which is 30.2 percent over the period of time studied here. That means the average attrition rate is $\bar{y} = 0.302$. If $\hat{y}_i^* \geq 0.302$, then $\hat{y}_i = 1$; otherwise $\hat{y}_i = 0$.

The population as a whole can be split into four groups according to Figure 3.1. The figure shows that the four groups are distinguished

Figure 3.1
Sensitivity and Specificity

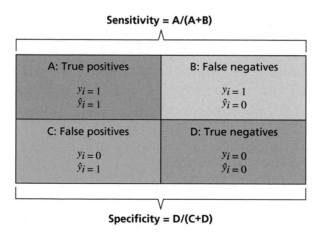

NOTE: *Sensitivity* is the fraction of true attriters that is correctly predicted, and *specificity* is the fraction of true nonattriters that is correctly predicted. A perfect prediction algorithm would attain both a sensitivity and a specificity of 1.

based on the true versus the predicted values for the individual. When the true and predicted values are both positive (or equal to 1, corresponding here to attrition), the individual is a true positive (box A). When the true value is positive but the predicted value is negative, the individual is a false negative (box B). Sensitivity refers to the true positive detection rate—the ratio of A to A+B. One goal of a prediction algorithm is to maximize the number of individuals in box A and minimize the number in box B.

Analogously, when the true and predicted values are both negative (or 0, corresponding here to not attriting), the individual is a true negative (box D). When the true value is negative, but the prediction is positive, the individual is a false positive (box C). Specificity corresponds to the ratio of C to C+D. Another goal of prediction is to maximize the number of individuals in box D and minimize the number in box C.

When the algorithm perfectly categorizes all individuals into either box A or D, then it perfectly identifies attriters from nonattriters, and both sensitivity and specificity are equal to 1.

The Relevance of Sensitivity and Specificity: A Conceptual Example

Both high sensitivity and high specificity are important for predictive models to be useful in practice. This is because a combination of high sensitivity and low specificity (or vice versa) can be caused by nearly all attriters being associated with one observable characteristic X and most, but not all, nonattriters also being associated with that characteristic X. Then, the prediction from a regression model would say that everyone with characteristic X has a high probability of attrition. The regression model has identified nearly all attriters (high sensitivity) but has mis-identified a high fraction of nonattriters (low specificity). In practice, then, characteristic X is a poor variable to use when thinking about policy recommendations because it does not actually distinguish the two groups.

To see more clearly why this is a potential problem for finding policy-relevant variables, consider a concrete example. Among the whole population, suppose 90 percent are type X and 10 percent are not. Among those who are type X, 90 percent attrite. Among those who are not type X, only 40 percent attrite. The population can be categorized into four groups as follows:

1. X-type attriters: 81 percent
2. Other attriters: 4 percent
3. X-type nonattriters: 9 percent
4. Other nonattriters: 6 percent.

The overall attrition rate is 85 percent; 95 percent of attriters are of type X, and 60 percent of nonattriters are type X. If we predicted attrition based only on the characteristic X, all Xs would be assigned 1 ("attrite") and all others would be assigned 0 ("do not attrite"). We can relabel the groups above based on whether they truly attrite and whether they are predicted to do so:

1. Attrite = 1, predict = 1: 81 percent
2. Attrite = 1, predict = 0: 4 percent
3. Attrite = 0, predict = 1: 9 percent
4. Attrite = 0, predict = 0: 6 percent.

Referring to the formulae in Figure 3.1, the sensitivity would be 95 percent, while the specificity is only 40 percent. This means the number of nonattriters would be cut by 60 percent under a policy that prevents type-X candidates from accessing—even though that policy would also eliminate most attriters. Whether such a policy is cost-effective depends on the relative benefit of false positives (eliminating nonattriters) versus false negatives (accessing an attriter), but the point is that such a policy can be a somewhat blunt instrument. Sensitivity is not the only parameter that is relevant in calculating a policy's cost-effectiveness, and, all else equal, higher specificity would be beneficial, just as higher sensitivity would be.

This overly simple example highlights why specificity must be considered in conjunction with sensitivity: to ensure that variables that apparently can screen out attriters do not also unduly screen out non-attriters. The analysis below will therefore seek to identify groups of variables that achieve a balance of high sensitivity and high specificity, and to discuss why the usefulness of certain variables might vary across services or across different timings of attrition.

Empirical Results

To compare sensitivity and specificity across different sets of variables, probit regressions were run separately for each group of observable variables listed in Table 2.1. The sensitivity and specificity were calculated for each group separately, and then for a single regression combining all variables. This was done to observe which variables contribute most to the predictive power of the full regression, which can, in turn, suggest hypotheses about why some variables matter more than others. This method was used for each separate service and for each separate benchmark outcome—that is, three-month, six-month, 12-month, and 36-month attrition, as well as 36-month attrition conditional on serving at least six months. (In other words, each individual has a separate prediction for whether they would attrite by three months, by six months, by 12 months, by 36 months, or after six months, based on their service branch and observable characteristics.) The different time frames allow for development of hypotheses regarding why different characteristics would be associated with attrition at different points in the first term, and why attrition at certain points in the term may be more predictable than at others.

The sensitivity and specificity calculations derive from predicted probabilities, which are fractions between 0 and 1. The extent to which the distribution of predicted probabilities for attriters overlaps with that for nonattriters is a determinant of whether the predictions can attain high sensitivity and specificity. When the distributions largely overlap, it means that many attriters and nonattriters have similar predicted probabilities, and therefore predictions may produce many false positives or false negatives. It is therefore beneficial to visualize the distributions first, to contextualize the sensitivities and specificities plotted below.

Figure 3.2 shows the distribution of predicted probabilities of 36-month attrition for each service, based on regressions using all variables listed in Table 2.1.[4] For each service, the distribution of attriters is shifted to the right, with a heavier right tail, compared with the distribution for nonattriters. This indicates that attriters, on average, have larger predicted probabilities and also that the service members with the highest predicted probabilities tend to be attriters. Nevertheless, the distributions largely overlap, indicating that the majority of attrit-

Figure 3.2
Distributions of Predicted Probabilities of 36-Month Attrition, by Service

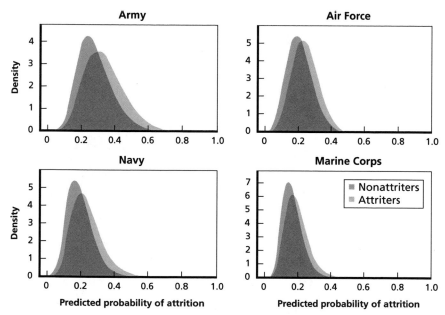

SOURCE: DMDC data merged to BLS data at the county level.
NOTE: Predictions are from probit regressions using all variables listed in Table 2.1.

_____

[4]   For the sake of brevity, plots of predicted probabilities for other attrition cutoffs are not shown, but they are qualitatively similar to those in Figure 3.2.

ers and nonattriters have similar probabilities. Only those with very high or very low probabilities can be correctly classified as true attriters or true nonattriters with a high degree of accuracy.

In light of these observations, it is unlikely that regressions can attain sensitivities or specificities near 100 percent. Figure 3.3 shows that this is indeed true. The figure shows the sensitivity and specificity for regressions predicting attrition by 36 months (the results for other timings were qualitatively similar and are excluded for the sake of space). Solid circles indicate sensitivity, and open circles indicate 1-minus-specificity. The latter is used as an alternative to the specificity itself to provide for an easier visual interpretation of the results: The closer sensitivity is to 1 and the closer (1–specificity) is to 0, then the wider the line between them, and the better the variables are at distinguishing those who attrite from those who do not. When the circles are perfectly overlapping, it means the regression variables predicted

Figure 3.3
Sensitivity and Specificity of Variables in Predicting 36-Month Attrition

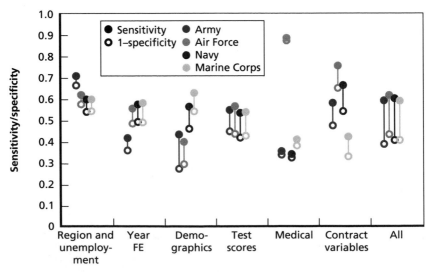

SOURCE: Author's analysis from DMDC data merged to BLS data at the county level.
NOTE: FE = fixed effects (dummy variables).

attrition in the same proportion for the whole sample and did not at all distinguish attriters from everyone else.

Over all of the services, the geographic/unemployment variables and the medical screening variables have the least ability to distinguish attriters and nonattriters, with FY fixed effects close behind. Geographic region and local unemployment have relatively high sensitivity but low specificity, while, for medical tests, the opposite is true. (An exception is the Air Force, for which medical test results have high sensitivity and low specificity.) In general, then, to attain a desirable balance of high sensitivity and high specificity, geographic and medical variables need to be combined with other observable information.

Demographics, test scores, and contract variables achieve a better balance of sensitivity and specificity. Across all services, test scores have a stable balance of 50-percent to 60-percent sensitivity and specificity. In other words, test scores alone can accurately predict just over half of attriters and nonattriters in any service and at any point in the first term. One interpretation of such similarities across services is that at least some attrition is due entirely to quantifiable skills and that some fraction of recruits lacks the skills necessary to succeed in any military service. The fact that sensitivity and specificity of test scores are so similar across services suggests that skill mismatch in terms of occupations is not the cause. For example, if attrition of low-AFQT individuals were due to these individuals being assigned to occupations that do not fit their skills, we would expect this problem to be more severe in some services than in others. Instead, the results imply that there is some stable fraction of individuals who are simply unable to perform at a sufficiently high level to retain them in service.

Demographics yield more varied results. The demographics do a relatively poorer job at predicting Army outcomes (sensitivity is reduced below 50 percent) but a better job at predicting Navy and Marine Corps outcomes (sensitivity and specificity are both near or above 50 percent). These differences across services are potentially important but may have multiple causes. First, the services recruit different types of individuals, as shown in Table 2.2. Second, the services have different policies and missions that may differentially affect the attrition rates of different types of individuals, as well as the points in which the services make most of their cuts.[5]

For variables characterizing the contract, the Army and Navy show balanced sensitivity and specificity, both around 50 to 60 percent. For the Air Force, contract variables have higher sensitivity, more than 70 percent, but specificity is around 40 percent. The Marine Corps shows the opposite pattern. These results show that the characteristics of a contract can predict a sizeable amount of attrition, but that contracts are a coarse summary of a recruit's characteristics, meaning that the predictions may be especially poor if certain aspects of a contract are very correlated with attrition. The Air Force, for example, uses relatively few occupational categories in the contract, and nearly 100 percent of attriters are placed in the Non-Occupational category—while most, but not all, nonattriters are placed in this category as well. As with medical variables, the apparently high sensitivity and low specificity of Air Force contract variables is, therefore, a mechanical result of the regression algorithm predicting attrition based primarily on a single categorical variable.[6]

Although different sets of variables perform better for certain services or for certain attrition outcomes, these differences even out somewhat when all variables are combined. Regressions with the complete set of variables provide the best balance of sensitivity and specificity, with the results being consistent across services—both sensitivity and specificity are around 55 percent to 60 percent in all cases. Thus, the complete set of variables provides the most robust possibilities for prediction, but, as discussed below, there is still enough room for improvement that relying on these predictions alone may not be a cost-effective basis for recruitment policy.

---

[5]   Although the results are not shown, Army attrition is relatively more predictable from demographic characteristics early in the first term compared with later.

[6]   In other words, Non-Occupational job assignment is similar to characteristic X in the conceptual example above.

CHAPTER FOUR

Marginal Effects of Recruit Characteristics

In this chapter, the marginal effect of various characteristics on attrition at different points in the first term is examined. The marginal effect gives the increase or decrease in the probability of attrition when an individual has a given characteristic versus when they do not. Rather than tabulating overall differences in attrition based on a given characteristic, this analysis shows differences in attrition conditional on all other characteristics. Based on the results of the previous section, the probit regressions have the best sensitivity/specificity balance when all variables are included; thus, these marginal effects are calculated from regressions using all of the available variables.

As for predicted probabilities of attrition, marginal change in probabilities is calculated using the cumulative normal distribution. Unlike for predicted probabilities, marginal effects condition on data for the whole population rather than for a single individual. As elaborated above, each individual i is recorded as a $1(k + 1)$ vector of variables x_i. If variable j is a categorical (dummy) variable, let $x^1_{i,-j}$ be the vector of data, where variable j is set to equal 1 and all other variables remain at their true values; $x^0_{i,-j}$ is defined analogously.[1] With N total individuals in the sample, the estimated marginal effect of characteristic j on attrition is then calculated as follows:

$$\text{margin}_j = \frac{1}{N} \sum_{i=1}^{N} \Phi\left(\widehat{\beta}' x^1_{i,-j}\right) - \Phi\left(\widehat{\beta}' x^0_{i,-j}\right).$$

---

[1] In particular, marginal effects are being calculated for each person at the true value of all other characteristics and averaged across all individuals. They are not calculated at the mean value for the whole population.

The particular variables discussed below were chosen because they have been heavily examined in prior research, because the patterns are surprising or illuminating, or because the services differ in policies that may influence attrition based on a particular variable.

Female Attrition

Gender is one such variable with respect to which services have different policies. Unlike the other services, the Marine Corps segregated basic training during the window of analysis in this study. Until recently, one justification for this segregation was that combat positions were closed to women and the majority of Marine Corps jobs involve ground combat. With the recent change in policy allowing women to serve in combat positions, the Marine Corps eventually integrated boot camp, but not without some debate about whether the change would be appropriate or effective (Philipps and Gibbons-Neff, 2019; Schehl, 2016; Germano, 2018).

For the period studied here, women were not allowed in combat positions, so these changes are not germane to the analysis. Instead, the question is whether segregated basic training might have an impact on female attrition, either during training or later in the first term. Figure 4.1 shows the marginal effect of being female for each service and each attrition timing benchmark. The Marine Corps does not stand out from the other services. In the first three months, across all services, women have a 1-to-3–percentage point–higher probability of attrition than males. In the first six months, the results across services start to disperse, but the marginal effect is still between 3 and 7 percentage points. Beyond six months, however, the services are quite different. The Army has especially high marginal effects: Compared to males, females have a 13 percent–higher probability of attrition between months 7 and 36. In the Navy, the difference in months 7 to 36 is zero, indicating that any sex-based differences in attrition occur early in the first term. In the Air Force and Marine Corps, the difference is around 3 to 4 percentage points.

The results suggest that segregated training is not necessarily a factor in female attrition, although there are also service-based differences in the standards women must meet during training, and these differences could offset any effect of segregated training. Whether coed training would make a difference in Marine Corps attrition depends on which service provides the appropriate counterfactual and how, exactly, such standards for women are adjusted when coed units are introduced. Based on the evidence from the other services, there would be little difference in three-month attrition. But after six months, attrition could go up or down. If the Navy provides the closest model for how women in the Marine Corps would be trained in coed units, then it is possible that attrition later in the first term could go down.

If anything, Figure 4.1 highlights the Army as an outlier in terms of female attrition. The especially large marginal effect for seven-through-36-month attrition implies that the Army most differs from the other services in the integration of females into its units once training has concluded. This high female attrition is the subject of much

Figure 4.1
Marginal Effect of Being Female on First-Term Attrition

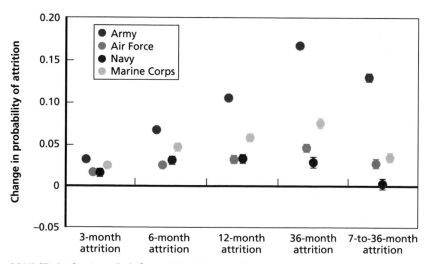

SOURCE: Author's analysis from DMDC data and BLS data merged at the county level.
NOTE: Vertical bars represent 95-percent confidence intervals.

recent research exploring its various causes and pathways.[2] Future research may seek to further understand how institutional, personal, and peer characteristics interact to influence female attrition.

Attrition Among Recruits with Less Than a High School Diploma

Education has often been examined in past research on first-term attrition. The lack of a high school diploma is one characteristic used to distinguish low- from high-quality recruits, and it also influences the occupation offered to recruits. It may, therefore, influence attrition directly, as a proxy for a recruit's skills, or indirectly, due to differences in attrition by occupation.

Figure 4.2 shows the marginal effect of having no high school diploma at accession, compared with having at least a diploma, GED, or equivalent. There is no substantive effect on three-month attrition, indicating that lack of a diploma does not affect a recruit's success during basic training and that none of the services make cuts early on based on anything correlated with having a diploma.

After three months, lack of a diploma implies a moderate increase of 1 to 4 percentage points on attrition in the Army, Air Force, and Marine Corps (although this is not statistically significant for the Air Force). The Navy is an exception, with an increase of 10 percent, almost entirely due to attrition after the sixth month of service.

GED Attrition

Research in labor economics affirms that GED holders and high school graduates are not equivalent and has highlighted differences in so-called "soft skills" as the main factor. Despite having roughly equivalent academic credentials to high school graduates, GED holders

---

[2]   These pathways include the importance of female leaders and the effects of sexual assault and other negative experiences (Asch, Miller, and Weinberger, 2016; Morral, Gore, and Schell, 2015; Daniel et al., 2019).

Figure 4.2
Marginal Effect of Having Less Than a High School Diploma on First-Term Attrition

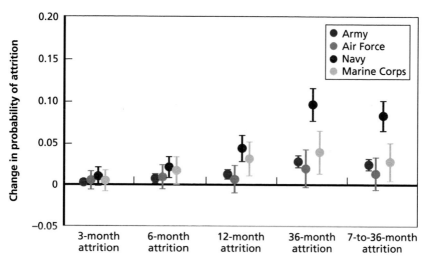

SOURCE: Author's analysis from DMDC data and BLS data merged at the county level.
NOTE: Vertical bars represent 95-percent confidence intervals.

are found to perform very similarly to high school dropouts; the conclusion of recent research is that GED holders lack the character and noncognitive skills necessary to succeed on the labor market (Heckman, Humphries, and Kautz, 2014). Translating these findings to the military, one would expect that GED holders would attrite at higher rates than others, and that the impact of any differences in soft skills might manifest later in the first term, when recruits' ability to discharge their duties are fully observed. Indeed, as Laurence (2014) documents, extensive research on GED and other alternative credential holders shows that they consistently attrite at higher rates than those with high school diplomas.

Figure 4.3 shows the marginal effect of a GED on attrition, compared with having a high school diploma. Unlike lack of a high school diploma, the effects based on a GED are more similar across services and more equal over time in terms of proportional impact on the baseline attrition rate. The effect on three-month attrition is statistically

Figure 4.3
Marginal Effect of Having a GED or Equivalent on First-Term Attrition

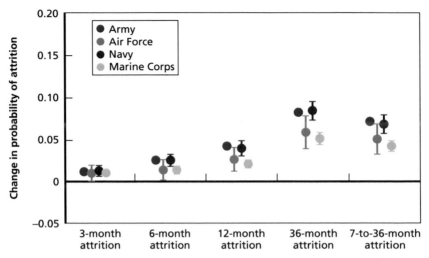

SOURCE: Author's analysis from DMDC data and BLS data merged at the county level.
NOTE: Vertical bars represent 95-percent confidence intervals.

significant, at around 1 percentage point for all services. Given a base-line of roughly 5-percent attrition in the first three months, this is a 20-percent increase in attrition. The effects are slightly larger at the six-month level, but the biggest effects are seen after six months. In the Air Force and Marine Corps, GEDs imply a 4– or 5–percentage point increase in attrition. For the Army and Navy, the effects are just over 8 percentage points at the 36-month mark. Across the services, these effects translate to 20-percent to 25-percent increases on the baseline attrition rates. Thus, the biggest absolute increase of attrition is late in the term, but the proportional impact is roughly constant across the entire first term.

Unfavorable Entrance National Agency Check Attrition

Like the GED, unfavorable ENTNAC results may indicate something about a recruit's character that is otherwise unobservable. Unfavorable information includes indications that the individual is untrustworthy or has an arrest record (although not a felony conviction). Studies of preenlistment characteristics show that an applicant's history can be a predictor of recidivism—for example, in cases of drug use (White et al., 2016) or behavioral issues. In this sense, an unfavorable ENTNAC may serve as a warning that a recruit will eventually separate for reasons related to the flags on their background check.

Like attrition of GED holders, attrition of recruits with unfavorable ENTNAC results does not occur uniformly throughout the first term. Figure 4.4 shows that such recruits have no differential propensity to separate in the first six months, and even a slightly lower tendency to attrite in the Army. The marginal effect ticks up sharply by 36 months, with the effect ranging from an additional 2.7 percentage points in the Army to 6.4 percentage points in the Navy. On the baseline attrition rate, this is an increase of 10 percent to 25 percent.

Figure 4.4
Marginal Effect of Unfavorable ENTNAC Result on First-Term Attrition

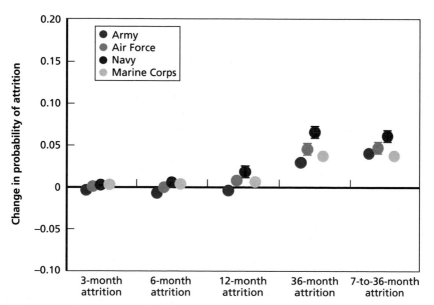

SOURCE: Author's analysis from DMDC data and BLS data merged at the county level.
NOTE: Vertical bars represent 95-percent confidence intervals.

The change in the marginal effect of ENTNAC over the course of a recruit's first term supports a theory that ENTNAC waivers predict an inability to meet standards of performance after the first assignment rather than during training. What cannot be determined from these data is whether this timing is due to a mismatch between these recruits' skills/interests and their occupational assignment, or because these recruits eventually get into trouble and are discharged, or for another reason. Recent research implies that the reasons may be a mixture of the two. Lundquist, Pager, and Strader (2018) find that recruits with felony waivers are more likely to commit crimes during their term of service and are more likely to be killed in action—but are also promoted more quickly than other enlistees. They hypothesize that some of these effects are because felony-waiver recruits are assigned to infantry at higher rates, suggesting a connection between high-risk behavior, occupational assignment, and first-term outcomes.

Attrition of Married Recruits

Past research finds mixed effects of marriage. Buddin (2005) concludes that married recruits are less likely to attrite during DEP and are also less likely to complete the first term—but are more likely to reenlist if they do complete the term. Orvis et al. (2018) also find that married recruits are less likely to complete the first term, although not by much; formerly married recruits have a larger propensity to attrite. Military service also interacts with the probability of getting married or divorced. Hogan and Seifert (2010) find that marriage itself is more common for young active-duty military service members, compared with similar civilians, and that the odds of divorce are also greater after two years of service, compared with civilians. Carter and Wozniak (2018) show that relocations, such as permanent change of station moves, are strongly associated with increased marriage rates. Together, the research suggests that the decision to get married and stay married and the decision to serve and remain in service are intertwined.

The reasons for the pattern of marriage and early attrition are not necessarily obvious. Recruits who are married at the time of accession clearly face a specific set of pressures for work-life balance. But to balance these pressures, the military does offer certain benefits to married soldiers in the form of larger housing allowances and several family benefits on military bases. There may be some juggling of family and work that occurs early in the first term, leading to greater attrition for married recruits than for single soldiers who have no spouse or children. But it is not necessarily obvious whether married recruits would continue to attrite at higher or lower rates than single recruits, once they have figured out their daily routines and balanced the expectations of their jobs with the expectations of their families.

Figure 4.5 shows the marginal effect of being married at accession on first-term attrition in the analytic sample used in this study. The patterns affirm the previous findings that marriage is generally associated with higher attrition, but they show that this higher propensity is only early in the first term. Across all services, three-to-12-month attrition for married recruits is higher than for single recruits. Except for the Air Force, the same is true of 36-month attrition—but this is

Figure 4.5
Marginal Effect of Being Married at Accession on First-Term Attrition

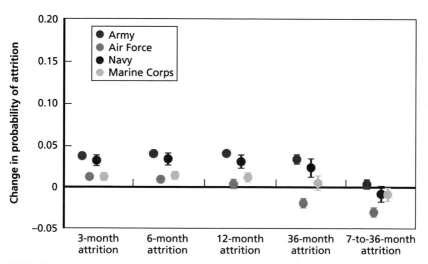

SOURCE: Author's analysis from DMDC data and BLS data merged at the county level.
NOTE: Vertical bars represent 95-percent confidence intervals.

entirely due to attrition before six months. Conditional on staying past six months, differential attrition of married recruits in every service is either zero or negative.

The ordering of the effect across services is also stable: The Army has the highest effect, 3.8 to 4.1 percentage points for three-, six-, and 12-month attrition, followed by the Navy and Marine Corps. The Air Force has the lowest, at 1.2 percentage points for three months to a statistically nonsignificant 0.3 percentage points at 12 months. For the seven-to-36-month mark, the effect ranges from a nonsignificant 0.3 percentage points for the Army to –3 percentage points for the Air Force.

On a baseline of 20-percent to 25-percent attrition, the negative marginal effect in months 7 to 36 is not huge in substantive terms. But overall, the results support the notion that married recruits face a learning curve during the early months that can pay off for those who last through training. Future research would be necessary to affirm this theory by examining the reasons for married recruit separation to determine whether it appears to be primarily a choice made by the recruits themselves or whether married recruits are cut at higher rates during boot camp for some other reason. What kind of support do married recruits need to stay through training? And if programs turn "attriters" into "stayers," would they then complete their terms at similar rates to everyone else? The answers to these questions would provide insight into whether programs aimed at supporting new, married recruits would be cost-effective in mitigating attrition.

One complicating factor in this story is that single recruits may get married and married recruits may get divorced after accession. In fact, the benefits provided to married couples incentivize marriage for those recruits who are already in long-term relationships (Lundquist and Xu, 2014). Because the timing of marriage, divorce, and attrition are potentially interrelated, it would be difficult to compare already-married recruits directly to recruits who stay single. More-sophisticated methods, such as propensity-score matching, could address this question.

Attrition of Enlistees with No Delayed Entry Program

Entering the DEP before accession is extremely common. According to Table 2.2, the majority of recruits who eventually access will go through DEP. Past studies emphasize the distinction between DEP attrition (in which an individual enters DEP but fails to show up for training) and first-term attrition conditional on DEP (in which an individual enters DEP and eventually separates sometime after accession). The longer an individual spends in DEP, the higher the probability of DEP attrition (Buddin, 2005; Orvis et al., 2018). This is because longer DEP gives recruits more time to reverse their decision, for any reason. Conversely, longer DEP also correlates with a lower probability of attrition during training or later, conditional on actually entering active service.[3]

Figure 4.6 shows that recruits who enter directly from the contract (i.e., those with no DEP) have a small but generally positive increase in the probability of attrition. The effect on three-month attrition is very small and statistically insignificant. In the Navy, the effect grows after that, from 1.9 percentage points at six months to 2.9 percentage points in the first 12 months, remaining constant at the 36-month mark. The other services have muted effects; for the Army and Air Force, the result is never statistically significant, and for the Marine Corps, there is a 1.2–percentage point increase in probability after six months. Compared with the other characteristics examined here, these effects are less notable. But they also affirm the theory that DEP has a two-sided effect on attrition, depending on whether an individual completes DEP in the first place.

One explanation for the patterns in Figure 4.6 is a selection effect. The data include only accession, so those who attrite during DEP are not observed. As noted above, those recruits who enter DEP and still show up to basic training have had time to reconsider their decision and, therefore, may have a higher level of commitment than those who went straight to basic training. Thus, Figure 4.6 may be showing the residual, excess attrition for those who did not have time to reconsider

---

[3]   See, for example, Orvis et al. (2018), Tables 2.4 and 2.5. Buddin (2005) does not find any effect of DEP on later outcomes.

Figure 4.6
Marginal Effect of Entering Service Without DEP on First-Term Attrition

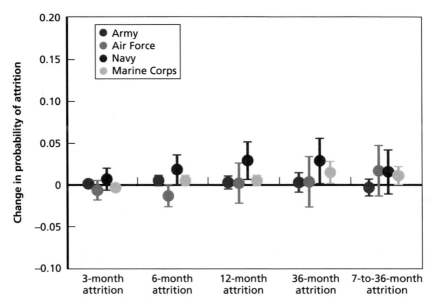

SOURCE: Author's analysis from DMDC data and BLS data merged at the county level.
NOTE: Vertical bars represent 95-percent confidence intervals.

their decision to enter military service. However, the patterns do not hold for every service or for the period of basic training, so the lessons to be drawn are limited.

Besides the selection effect, DEP may also reduce attrition because it can be used to generate a better match between a recruit and their skill set. For example, recruits may enter DEP partly because they want to wait for a preferable occupation. They may also enter DEP to work to meet fitness standards, or to graduate from high school. Each of these reasons for entering DEP may result in a recruit who is more pre-pared for service and, therefore, more likely to succeed.

CHAPTER FIVE

Discussion

Chapters Three and Four provided evidence that the correlation between recruits' characteristics and their probability of attrition vary over time throughout the first term of service. This variation is true in every service, despite some service-specific idiosyncrasies for particular characteristics. The predictive power of all variables combined also varies across the first term, as does the marginal effect on attrition for individual characteristics conditional on all other observables.

In this chapter, the author considers the relevance of these findings for policies intended to mitigate attrition and examines the likely costs and benefits of policies that change the mixture of recruits who enter—for example, by contracting differentially based on applicants' observable probability of attrition. Next is a discussion of the practicality of such policies relative to alternative policies that address post-accession causes of attrition by improving recruits' fit, experiences, and support networks throughout the first term.

Individual Versus Population Attrition Projections

The results above indicate that, at best, a given individual can accurately be predicted as an attriter or nonattriter 60 percent of the time. That is better than a coin flip, but far from perfect. The results also show that predictions are better made by considering all available information together rather than focusing on single characteristics. These observations imply that recruitment policies focusing on single characteristics, as opposed to population-level analyses, could be quite costly.

The costs arise from the fact that most recruits do not attrite, and so any policy that caps the number of recruits with a particular high-attrition characteristic will inevitably bar more nonattriters than it does attriters. In more-technical terms, this is Type I error.

To see how this sort of misidentification would be potentially costly, consider the following simplified cost calculation, based on a hypothetical policy in which the military enlists only those applicants who are predicted not to attrite, based on the prediction described above. For the sake of illustration, suppose the services used the predictions calculated here and decided to limit the number of contracts offered to predicted three-month attriters (i.e., those in boxes A and C of Figure 3.1).[1] Order-of-magnitude costs and benefits of this policy can be calculated using some stylized assumptions.

To begin, Enns (2012) provides cost estimates for Army and Navy attrition in FY 2008. Those services' three-month attrition rates, roughly corresponding to the time of boot camp, are, respectively, 5.2 percent and 6.3 percent. Based on the sensitivities in Figure 3.2, this policy would avoid enlisting, respectively, 65 percent and 67 percent of all attriters. Based on the cost estimates in Enns (2012), that would have saved the Army $37 million and the Navy $20.1 million in FY 2008 alone.

If the services were to invest in better predictive models, these numbers could be converted into marginal benefits of increased predictive power. Using Enns' numbers a different way, in FY 2008 a 1–percentage point increase in sensitivity would save the Army $571,000 and the Navy $300,000 through the avoidance of accessions that separate within three months. In terms of recruiting numbers, the averages in Table 2.2 indicate that, over the period studied here, each 1–percentage point increase in sensitivity would have saved the Army from enlisting 38 individuals every year who would attrite within three months; it would have saved the Air Force 15, the Navy 24, and the Marine Corps 17.

---

[1] As described in Chapter Three, a recruit is a predicted three-month attriter if their predicted probability of three-month attrition is higher than the average three-month attrition rate for that recruit's service branch.

Whether or not these seem like substantial savings, they miss a major piece of the puzzle: the false positives. By eliminating all predicted three-month attriters, the services would also have incorrectly barred 39 percent of Army and 41 percent of Navy nonattriters (based on the specificities in Figure 3.2). Because most enlistees are nonattriters, this is a huge reduction in the size of the active force—more than one-third of the total. It would not be possible to make up for this loss by finding recruits who have high predicted probabilities of retention. If the services were to follow a recruitment policy based on predicted three-month attrition over the time period studied here, every 1–percentage point increase in specificity would save the Army from needlessly barring 692 nonattriting recruits from enlistment; the Air Force would save 288, the Navy 352, and the Marine Corps 300. Gibson and Hackenbracht (2014) cite a marginal cost of $75,000 for new recruits as of FY 2013; using this number, the marginal benefit of increased sensitivity translates to $51.9 million for the Army, $21.6 million for the Air Force, $26.4 million for the Navy, and $22.5 million for the Marine Corps.

These rough calculations show that the marginal benefit of increased specificity is far higher than that of increased sensitivity. Given the three-month attrition rates in Table 2.2, this example policy will not be cost-effective unless the benefit of one fewer attriter is worth the cost of roughly eight fewer nonattriters. The costs of false positives would need to be very low relative to the cost of a false negative.

This illustration shows that it may be difficult to mitigate first-term attrition by focusing on individual recruits' characteristics. A population-level approach may be better, in which combinations of characteristics are determined in order to minimize cost while maintaining the current size of the force and having minimal impact on current levels of attrition. Using the whole package of recruit characteristics rather than focusing on individual variables provides more power in prediction models.

Orvis et al. (2018) develop one such model, an interactive Army recruitment tool that allows for cost comparisons between different recruitment regimes and accounts for how changes in recruitment might have ripple effects on attrition through DEP, training, and into the first term. The recruitment cost calculations come from another model, the Recruiting Resource Model of Knapp et al. (2018), which analyzes Army recruitment regimes with accessions as the primary outcome and calculates successful accessions based on inputs including local unemployment rates and the Army's television advertising spending.

Despite the power of such models, predictions using characteristics at accession can go only so far. The amount of information available at the time of recruitment is of limited use. With upward of 40 percent of attrition outcomes being unpredictable based on accession-level observables, it is clear that a major cause of attrition relates to factors that either are unobservable or occur after accession. These causes might be called *fit* or a *taste* for military life, and they could relate to the service as a whole, to a particular occupation, or to a particular unit. The point is that much information is revealed *ex-post*, and research findings must link these pathways to the characteristics that can be observed during recruitment.

A starting point is to determine why the services have such different attrition rates. As Figure 2.2 showed, the services differ much more in attrition rates after the first six months, when training is complete and enlistees are assigned to their first units. Some of these differences in attrition may be due to different mixtures of recruit characteristics. But some may be due to different degrees of fit, or different expectations for recruit behavior. As a simple exploration, consider the predicted 36-month attrition rate in each of the service branches using the coefficients from regressions based on other services' data. This shows the predicted attrition if the recruits in one service were to attrite with the same propensity as identical recruits in a different branch. Table 5.1 shows the predicted attrition rates using regression coefficients from the Army (which has the highest 36-month attrition rate) and the Marine Corps (which has the lowest). The regressions use all variables from Table 2.1.

Comparing the true rates in Table 2.2 with the predicted counterfactual rates in Table 5.1, it is clear that service-specific differences explain much of the attrition rate. Services' actual rates of attrition tend to be lower than those predicted using Army or Marine Corps

Table 5.1
Predicted Attrition Rates Based on Regression Coefficients from Army and Marine Corps

Variable	Army	Air Force	Navy	Marine Corps
36-month attrition (percentage)				
Actual	29.7	23.1	23.6	18.5
Using Army coefficients	—	36.4	28.9	35.8
Using Marine Corps coefficients	39.0	20.6	32.9	—

SOURCE: Author's calculation from DMDC data merged to BLS data at the county level. Actual attrition rates are taken from Table 2.2.

regression coefficients. For instance, the Army actually has a 29.7-percent 36-month attrition rate; if those same soldiers were to be placed in the Marine Corps, their predicted attrition rate would be 38.9 percent. Conversely, the Marine Corps has an actual 36-month attrition rate of 18.5 percent, but it would be predicted to be 35.8 percent if the same recruits were in the Army. The Air Force's and Navy's actual attrition rates are lower than the rates predicted by both Army and Marine Corps regression coefficients.

One interpretation is that people who fit one service would be poor fits in another, and the services do a good job of recruiting those who fit them best: Someone who makes a good soldier would be less likely to make a good marine, and vice versa. Another interpretation, almost an inversion of the first, is that the services have done a good job at minimizing attrition conditional on the recruit pool with which they are working. Both interpretations could be partly true. Fit depends on the expectations and culture of the particular service, but those expectations and that service-specific culture also adapt to the available recruits. The counterfactual attrition rates of Table 5.1 show that if all services had the same expectations, standards, and culture, then attrition rates might be quite a few percentage points higher.

Based on the evidence presented in this report, a promising approach to minimize attrition could be to focus on recruits during their times of greatest risk. Chapter Four shows some such conditions, such as being married at the beginning of the first term. More research would be required to uncover the reasons for differential attrition between different types of recruits at different points in time. This research should include an analysis of when and why attrition is due to *push* factors (e.g., the services cutting people) or *pull* factors (e.g., people deciding to leave).

Ideally, future research needs to allow for the prediction of attrition during the course of the first term rather than before it. This is important because policies addressing postaccession causes of attrition may be more cost-effective than changing the mixture of recruits. Such research would provide a missing piece of current models: the interactive effect of recruits' characteristics with their experiences after accession. Recent work has shed light on some of these potential attrition pathways. For example, research on peer effects shows that the exact mixture of recruits in a unit can have impacts on promotions, among other outcomes; the same could be true of attrition (Karaca-Mandic, Maestas, and Power, 2013). And some characteristics that are associated with attrition in general are also associated with superior performance in certain tasks. As noted above, recruits with criminal backgrounds are assigned to infantry at higher rates and may actually perform better than other recruits in that particular role, at least in terms of promotion time (Lundquist, Pager, and Strader, 2018).

Finally, and relatedly, future research needs to elucidate the currently unobservable causes of attrition. No study is able to predict close to 100 percent of attrition, which means other causes could explain quite a bit. Such causes could include unobservable characteristics, such as personality traits.[2] They could also include factors that arise after accession, such as changes in such characteristics as marital status, number of dependents, education, or health. They could also be experiential: for example, peer effects, relationships with senior enlisted service members, or effects of deployment. Research has already established that some of these factors are important correlates of attrition. Much work remains to be done to establish the pathways by which these factors might affect attrition, and how important they are.

---

[2]   Strictly speaking, personality traits are not unobservable, but they are not currently available to recruiters or to researchers.

CHAPTER SIX

Conclusion

This report is an analysis of first-term attrition across all military service branches at various points during the first contract: before three,
six, 12, and 36 months, and between seven and 36 months. It shows
that characteristics of individuals at the time of accession can reliably
predict up to 60 percent of those who will and will not attrite at each
point in time. It also shows that the relationship between particular
characteristics varies over time but that those relationships are often
similar across services.

By framing the research question in terms of the predictive power
of various variables, the author shows that despite fairly robust ability
to predict attrition, the problem of Type I error (or the misprediction
of nonattriters) introduces a practical issue that limits the usefulness
of preaccession predictions as part of screening during recruitment.
More data could improve the predictive power of all recruitment cost
models and would provide more-precise estimates of all outcomes of
interest. Helpful data would include characteristics that are not currently observable during the recruitment process, particularly variables
recording medical history, personality traits, and measures of character, such as grit and perseverance.

On the other hand, additional data on accession-level characteristics may go only so far. As evidence accumulates for major
postaccession causes of attrition, it will be increasingly beneficial to
invest in identifying the particular pathways by which first-term experiences interact with preaccession characteristics to improve existing
models and to develop new ways of predicting attrition throughout the

entire first term based on information from a recruit's entire trajectory, from application to separation.

Main Regression Results

Tables A.1 through A.5 show the regression coefficients for the main specifications described in the text. The marginal effects plotted in Chapter Four are calculated from these regressions. The sensitivity and specificity shown in the "All" category of Figure 3.3 are also calculated from these regressions. The tables show coefficients instead of marginal effects because some marginal effects are difficult to interpret on their own (for example, BMI-squared). Marginal effects for variables not discussed in Chapter Four are available from the author on request.

Table A.1
Probit Coefficients for Three-Month Attrition Based on Characteristics at Accession

	Army	Air Force	Marine Corps	Navy
County-level unemployment rate	−0.00577***	0.00183	0.000269	−0.000181
	(0.00161)	(0.00254)	(0.00246)	(0.00318)
American Samoa	−0.880***	−0.0906	−0.175	—
	(0.263)	(0.449)	(0.413)	
Micronesia	0.164	—	−0.0202	—
	(0.547)		(0.208)	
Marshall Islands	−0.505	—	—	—
	(0.426)			
Mariana Islands	0.835	—	0.0964	—
	(0.658)		(0.271)	
Puerto Rico	−0.0987*	−0.0760	−0.0147	0.0974
	(0.0433)	(0.0792)	(0.0989)	(0.0814)

Table A.1—Continued

	Army	Air Force	Marine Corps	Navy
Palau	−0.283	—	—	—
	(0.451)			
Minor outlying islands	0.372	—	—	—
	(0.272)			
U.S. Virgin Islands	−0.0946	−0.0223	−0.323	−0.0647
	(0.126)	(0.196)	(0.415)	(0.218)
Foreign country	−0.284	−0.169	−0.457	0.306
	(0.187)	(0.319)	(0.293)	(0.266)
Missing BLS match	−0.0140	−0.0292	−0.0164	−0.104
	(0.0324)	(0.0416)	(0.0546)	(0.0750)
West	−0.0654***	−0.140***	−0.0654***	−0.118***
	(0.00878)	(0.0132)	(0.0132)	(0.0164)
Midwest	0.0249**	0.00520	−0.00683	−0.0147
	(0.00840)	(0.0120)	(0.0122)	(0.0164)
Northeast	0.0126	−0.00717	0.0277*	−0.0403*
	(0.00992)	(0.0147)	(0.0134)	(0.0185)
Accession year				
2003	−0.173***	0.0112	−0.0260	0.0692
	(0.0208)	(0.0261)	(0.0322)	(0.0607)
2004	−0.0326	0.0535*	−0.0536	0.191**
	(0.0187)	(0.0254)	(0.0476)	(0.0708)
2005	−0.211***	−0.0144	−0.0695*	0.114*
	(0.0202)	(0.0286)	(0.0272)	(0.0563)
2006	−0.612***	0.0995***	−0.0436	0.161***
	(0.0186)	(0.0254)	(0.0271)	(0.0409)
2007	−0.445***	0.223***	−0.0938***	0.263***
	(0.0177)	(0.0253)	(0.0263)	(0.0367)
2008	−0.270***	0.0892***	−0.151***	0.234***
	(0.0171)	(0.0264)	(0.0266)	(0.0415)
2009	−0.182***	−0.148***	−0.0929**	0.305***
	(0.0188)	(0.0292)	(0.0297)	(0.0451)
2010	−0.186***	−0.104**	−0.121***	0.0256
	(0.0193)	(0.0327)	(0.0314)	(0.115)

Table A.1—Continued

	Army	Air Force	Marine Corps	Navy
2011	−0.258***	−0.177***	−0.205***	0.360***
	(0.0195)	(0.0348)	(0.0312)	(0.0390)
2012	−0.114***	−0.122***	−0.248***	0.245***
	(0.0189)	(0.0341)	(0.0309)	(0.0364)
2013	−0.113***	−0.0508	−0.209***	0.135***
	(0.0171)	(0.0335)	(0.0298)	(0.0339)
Accession month				
January	0.382***	0.0487*	−0.0658**	−0.203***
	(0.0160)	(0.0235)	(0.0221)	(0.0320)
February	0.422***	0.113***	0.227***	0.355***
	(0.0169)	(0.0221)	(0.0232)	(0.0275)
March	0.0789***	−0.0179	0.0457	0.0482
	(0.0191)	(0.0244)	(0.0245)	(0.0305)
April	0.343***	−0.0712**	−0.0328	−0.263***
	(0.0172)	(0.0252)	(0.0259)	(0.0331)
May	0.351***	0.172***	0.197***	0.153***
	(0.0172)	(0.0218)	(0.0221)	(0.0291)
July	0.324***	0.0296	−0.133***	−0.210***
	(0.0158)	(0.0241)	(0.0216)	(0.0278)
August	0.284***	0.156***	0.112***	0.0956***
	(0.0162)	(0.0210)	(0.0191)	(0.0265)
September	−0.0154	−0.0447	0.0411*	−0.0939**
	(0.0195)	(0.0249)	(0.0200)	(0.0291)
October	0.299***	−0.131***	−0.0567*	−0.274***
	(0.0175)	(0.0280)	(0.0246)	(0.0377)
November	0.203***	0.126***	0.154***	0.268***
	(0.0184)	(0.0224)	(0.0226)	(0.0294)
December	0.194***	−0.108***	0.103***	−0.0783*
	(0.0548)	(0.0264)	(0.0238)	(0.0357)
Female	0.345***	0.189***	0.286***	0.161***
	(0.00912)	(0.0121)	(0.0159)	(0.0154)
Black	−0.176***	−0.168***	−0.00703	−0.0886***
	(0.00973)	(0.0137)	(0.0153)	(0.0163)

Table A.1—Continued

	Army	Air Force	Marine Corps	Navy
Asian	−0.151***	−0.162***	−0.0830**	−0.128***
	(0.0191)	(0.0253)	(0.0276)	(0.0280)
American Indian	−0.0303	0.0151	0.0502	0.0174
	(0.0261)	(0.0354)	(0.0343)	(0.0190)
Other nonwhite	−0.0402**	−0.0869	−0.0389	−0.0468
	(0.0155)	(0.0487)	(0.0358)	(0.0410)
Hispanic	−0.185***	−0.152*	−0.147***	−0.136***
	(0.0114)	(0.0604)	(0.0172)	(0.0179)
Education				
Less than high school	0.0222	0.0496	0.0551	0.0959*
	(0.0205)	(0.0631)	(0.0724)	(0.0471)
GED or equivalent	0.123***	0.104*	0.119***	0.122***
	(0.00909)	(0.0500)	(0.0195)	(0.0276)
Associate's or some college	0.111***	0.0490	0.0838**	0.0857**
	(0.0135)	(0.0252)	(0.0309)	(0.0303)
Bachelor's	−0.0550	−0.149***	−0.106	−0.0425
	(0.0528)	(0.0417)	(0.0557)	(0.0381)
Postgraduate	0.0248	−0.345	N/A	−0.139
	(0.0756)	(0.298)		(0.164)
Divorced/separated	0.123***	0.0104	0.128	0.200**
	(0.0262)	(0.0778)	(0.0768)	(0.0664)
Married	0.343***	0.133***	0.135***	0.274***
	(0.0109)	(0.0188)	(0.0283)	(0.0275)
Widowed	0.227	N/A	0.978	0.241
	(0.225)		(0.674)	(0.564)
Number of children	−0.116***	−0.0976	−0.340***	−0.340***
	(0.0122)	(0.0556)	(0.0861)	(0.0588)
Married with children	−0.404***	−0.445***	−0.0957	−0.370***
	(0.0237)	(0.0737)	(0.119)	(0.0862)
21–25 years old	−0.0113	0.0308*	0.0544***	0.0319*
	(0.00801)	(0.0122)	(0.0131)	(0.0159)
26–30 years old	0.0828***	0.121***	0.231***	0.0861**
	(0.0140)	(0.0310)	(0.0310)	(0.0302)

Table A.1—Continued

	Army	Air Force	Marine Corps	Navy
31 or older	0.206***	0	0.312	0.270***
	(0.0200)	—	(0.166)	(0.0507)
Not a U.S. citizen	−0.211***	−0.337***	−0.124***	−0.228***
	(0.0210)	(0.0498)	(0.0301)	(0.0375)
Prior active-duty service	0.0223	0.178	0.262***	−0.0366
	(0.0764)	(0.106)	(0.0697)	(0.0742)
Signed contract during high school	0.0211*	−0.00931	−0.0325**	0.0434*
	(0.0107)	(0.0137)	(0.0126)	(0.0172)
Participated in youth program	0.132***	0.0486	0.0776***	0.0403
	(0.0149)	(0.0425)	(0.0191)	(0.0359)
No DEP	0.0113	−0.0772	−0.0400	0.0737
	(0.0284)	(0.0845)	(0.0354)	(0.0644)
4–6 months of DEP	−0.00335	−0.0440**	−0.0553**	−0.0220
	(0.0111)	(0.0159)	(0.0169)	(0.0223)
7–9 months of DEP	0.00127	−0.0979***	−0.0669***	−0.0471**
	(0.00924)	(0.0130)	(0.0123)	(0.0155)
10 or more months of DEP	0.0454**	−0.124***	−0.0884***	−0.0462*
	(0.0164)	(0.0191)	(0.0159)	(0.0223)
Accession rank				
E2	−0.184***	−0.135***	−0.166***	−0.429***
	(0.00754)	(0.0165)	(0.0125)	(0.0173)
E3	−0.278***	−0.217***	N/A	−0.289***
	(0.00990)	(0.0156)		(0.0182)
E4 or higher	−0.389***	N/A	−0.333	−0.909*
	(0.0508)		(0.538)	(0.410)
DoD occupational category				
Electronics	−0.0903***	−0.145	1.598***	0.0577
	(0.0153)	(0.369)	(0.467)	(0.193)
COMINT	−0.0888***	0.118	1.427*	0.0401
	(0.0119)	(0.135)	(0.712)	(0.337)
Health	−0.105***	−1.002***	N/A	−0.0149
	(0.0140)	(0.222)		(0.485)

Table A.1—Continued

	Army	Air Force	Marine Corps	Navy
Other technicians	−0.112***	−0.141	0.299	N/A
	(0.0182)	(0.160)	(0.542)	
Administrative	−0.0965***	−0.546***	N/A	−1.088***
	(0.0133)	(0.137)		(0.236)
Mechanical	−0.124***	−0.549***	N/A	0.0000602
	(0.0115)	(0.0903)		(0.0134)
Craftsworkers	−0.170***	−0.888**	N/A	−0.308
	(0.0223)	(0.303)		(0.405)
Service/supply	−0.0634***	−0.430***	0.952*	N/A
	(0.0112)	(0.105)	(0.444)	
Non-Occupational	0.00933	0.596***	0.490	N/A
	(0.0107)	(0.0499)	(0.282)	
ASVAB percentiles				
Arithmetic reasoning	−0.000167	0.00155***	0.000927*	0.00164***
	(0.000284)	(0.000405)	(0.000382)	(0.000432)
Auto information	−0.000364*	−0.00108***	−0.000712**	0.000129
	(0.000168)	(0.000235)	(0.000226)	(0.000317)
Coding speed	0.000863***	0.000317	0.00111***	0.000254
	(0.000162)	(0.000229)	(0.000218)	(0.000297)
Electronics information	−0.000114	0.000635	0.00194	−0.00200
	(0.00100)	(0.00129)	(0.00134)	(0.00171)
Mathematics	−0.00209***	−0.00208***	−0.00183***	−0.00214***
	(0.000170)	(0.000241)	(0.000235)	(0.000334)
Mech. comprehension	−0.000686***	−0.000949***	−0.000897***	−0.000817***
	(0.000119)	(0.000169)	(0.000169)	(0.000219)
Numerical operations	−0.00250***	−0.00204***	−0.00204***	−0.00186***
	(0.000256)	(0.000365)	(0.000340)	(0.000375)
Paragraph comprehension	−0.000385	−0.000459	−0.000753	0.00107
	(0.000410)	(0.000533)	(0.000571)	(0.000745)
Verbal expression	−0.00301***	0.00408	−0.000651	0.00153
	(0.000581)	(0.00462)	(0.000755)	(0.000807)
General science	0.000222	0.000894***	0.000480*	0.000803*
	(0.000176)	(0.000235)	(0.000242)	(0.000334)

Table A.1—Continued

	Army	Air Force	Marine Corps	Navy
Word knowledge	0.00167*	0.00332***	0.000708	0.00434***
	(0.000722)	(0.000933)	(0.000971)	(0.00127)
AFQT percentile	−0.000828	−0.00692***	−0.00328*	−0.00536***
	(0.00102)	(0.00164)	(0.00136)	(0.00139)
Failed ENTNAC	−0.0423***	0.0171	0.0451**	0.0288
	(0.0109)	(0.0220)	(0.0161)	(0.0274)
Color vision	−0.0110	0.0521	−0.0332	−0.0286
	(0.0163)	(0.0283)	(0.0215)	(0.0301)
PULHES: Physical capacity	0.0625***	0.00349	0.103***	0.0534
	(0.0157)	(0.0289)	(0.0221)	(0.0341)
PULHES: Upper extremities	0.119***	0.0376	0.115	0.0384
	(0.0351)	(0.0633)	(0.0612)	(0.0745)
PULHES: Lower extremities	0.203***	0.196***	0.179***	0.0597
	(0.0294)	(0.0490)	(0.0453)	(0.0611)
PULHES: Hearing	0.140***	0.00888	0.162***	0.167**
	(0.0238)	(0.0542)	(0.0396)	(0.0584)
PULHES: Vision	0.0693***	0.0710***	0.0599***	0.0683***
	(0.00740)	(0.0110)	(0.0109)	(0.0141)
PULHES: Psychiatric	−0.0232	0.188***	0.00338	−0.0223
	(0.0357)	(0.0484)	(0.0518)	(0.0808)
BMI	0.00567***	−0.00183	−0.00324*	−0.000736
	(0.000901)	(0.00169)	(0.00151)	(0.00186)
BMI-squared	0.000150**	0.000276*	0.000475***	0.000534***
	(0.0000498)	(0.000107)	(0.0000946)	(0.000139)
Constant	−1.385***	−1.858***	−1.873***	−1.357***
	(0.0326)	(0.0784)	(0.285)	(0.0545)
N	546,302	265,149	269,389	140,868
Pseudo-R^2	0.0633	0.0594	0.0340	0.0644

SOURCE: Author calculations from DMDC data merged with BLS data at the county level.

NOTES: Table shows coefficients from probit regressions with three-month attrition as the outcome variable. Standard errors are in parentheses. Base category June is omitted. Statistical significance is denoted by asterisks: * $p < 0.05$, ** $p < 0.01$, *** $p < 0.001$. N/A = not applicable.

Table A.2
Probit Coefficients for Six-Month Attrition Based on Characteristics at Accession

	Army	Air Force	Marine Corps	Navy
County-level unemployment rate	−0.00560***	0.000354	−0.00169	−0.00291
	(0.00127)	(0.00208)	(0.00211)	(0.00284)
American Samoa	−0.540***	−0.350	−0.135	—
	(0.129)	(0.443)	(0.323)	—
Micronesia	−0.347	—	−0.204	—
	(0.527)	—	(0.194)	—
Marshall Islands	−0.552	—	—	—
	(0.325)	—	—	—
Mariana Islands	0.940	—	−0.178	—
	(0.536)	—	(0.270)	—
Puerto Rico	−0.0878**	−0.0879	0.0519	0.112
	(0.0325)	(0.0647)	(0.0798)	(0.0717)
Palau	−0.418	—	−0.0418	—
	(0.351)	—	(0.461)	—
Minor outlying islands	0.197	—	—	—
	(0.238)	—	—	—
U.S. Virgin Islands	−0.168	−0.0340	−0.262	−0.175
	(0.104)	(0.163)	(0.326)	(0.193)
Foreign country	−0.474**	−0.385	−0.498	0.168
	(0.154)	(0.316)	(0.261)	(0.244)
Missing BLS match	0.0279	−0.0896*	−0.0331	−0.0662
	(0.0251)	(0.0352)	(0.0467)	(0.0618)
West	−0.0818***	−0.133***	−0.0729***	−0.143***
	(0.00691)	(0.0108)	(0.0112)	(0.0145)
Midwest	0.0115	−0.00504	−0.0164	−0.0353*
	(0.00666)	(0.0100)	(0.0104)	(0.0146)
Northeast	−0.0110	−0.0115	−0.0114	−0.0666***
	(0.00790)	(0.0123)	(0.0116)	(0.0164)
Accession year				
2003	−0.0146	−0.0566*	0.0264	0.124*
	(0.0167)	(0.0227)	(0.0275)	(0.0515)

Table A.2—Continued

	Army	Air Force	Marine Corps	Navy
2004	0.0830***	0.0571**	−0.0179	0.259***
	(0.0152)	(0.0217)	(0.0404)	(0.0605)
2005	−0.108***	0.00749	−0.0322	0.162***
	(0.0163)	(0.0241)	(0.0232)	(0.0483)
2006	−0.505***	0.0855***	−0.00940	0.159***
	(0.0146)	(0.0216)	(0.0232)	(0.0358)
2007	−0.345***	0.237***	−0.0643**	0.326***
	(0.0142)	(0.0215)	(0.0224)	(0.0319)
2008	−0.222***	0.0775***	−0.129***	0.255***
	(0.0140)	(0.0224)	(0.0227)	(0.0365)
2009	−0.117***	−0.126***	−0.0912***	0.286***
	(0.0153)	(0.0244)	(0.0255)	(0.0401)
2010	−0.106***	−0.00486	−0.151***	0.0313
	(0.0156)	(0.0270)	(0.0271)	(0.102)
2011	−0.139***	−0.0199	−0.255***	0.301***
	(0.0156)	(0.0282)	(0.0270)	(0.0346)
2012	−0.0519***	−0.0971***	−0.308***	0.243***
	(0.0154)	(0.0284)	(0.0267)	(0.0319)
2013	−0.0743***	0.00131	−0.234***	0.221***
	(0.0141)	(0.0279)	(0.0255)	(0.0295)
Accession month				
January	0.0282*	−0.0295	−0.107***	−0.268***
	(0.0116)	(0.0193)	(0.0186)	(0.0272)
February	0.105***	0.0317	0.139***	0.156***
	(0.0123)	(0.0185)	(0.0202)	(0.0245)
March	0.0357**	0.00933	0.0993***	−0.0154
	(0.0130)	(0.0196)	(0.0203)	(0.0262)
April	0.0302*	−0.0573**	−0.0525*	−0.309***
	(0.0126)	(0.0200)	(0.0219)	(0.0278)
May	0.0653***	0.0836***	0.121***	0.00892
	(0.0125)	(0.0183)	(0.0191)	(0.0256)
July	−0.0585***	−0.0400*	−0.189***	−0.269***
	(0.0116)	(0.0197)	(0.0181)	(0.0235)

Table A.2—Continued

	Army	Air Force	Marine Corps	Navy
August	−0.00946	0.0109	0.0187	−0.0544*
	(0.0116)	(0.0176)	(0.0164)	(0.0231)
September	−0.0195	−0.0688***	0.0555***	−0.0913***
	(0.0129)	(0.0202)	(0.0166)	(0.0244)
October	0.126***	−0.0604**	−0.114***	−0.282***
	(0.0125)	(0.0215)	(0.0209)	(0.0313)
November	0.157***	0.0489**	0.100***	0.0805**
	(0.0127)	(0.0187)	(0.0194)	(0.0261)
December	−0.0889*	−0.0236	0.120***	−0.150***
	(0.0434)	(0.0208)	(0.0199)	(0.0306)
Female	0.413***	0.188***	0.380***	0.231***
	(0.00732)	(0.0102)	(0.0135)	(0.0133)
Black	−0.179***	−0.165***	−0.0406**	−0.0586***
	(0.00770)	(0.0113)	(0.0133)	(0.0143)
American Indian	−0.0179	0.0189	0.00722	0.0376*
	(0.0202)	(0.0295)	(0.0301)	(0.0168)
Asian	−0.125***	−0.180***	−0.0693**	−0.115***
	(0.0146)	(0.0207)	(0.0233)	(0.0243)
Other nonwhite	−0.0229	−0.118**	−0.0403	−0.0269
	(0.0119)	(0.0413)	(0.0304)	(0.0357)
Hispanic	−0.189***	−0.124*	−0.157***	−0.143***
	(0.00891)	(0.0501)	(0.0146)	(0.0158)
Education				
Less than HS	0.0482**	0.0657	0.129*	0.149***
	(0.0157)	(0.0520)	(0.0597)	(0.0414)
GED or equivalent	0.154***	0.104*	0.111***	0.176***
	(0.00720)	(0.0423)	(0.0169)	(0.0245)
Associate or some college	0.109***	0.0269	0.0705**	0.0961***
	(0.0109)	(0.0210)	(0.0269)	(0.0269)
Bachelor's	0.104**	−0.168***	−0.0906	−0.0629
	(0.0360)	(0.0338)	(0.0464)	(0.0338)
Postgraduate	0.143**	−0.456	−0.414	−0.173
	(0.0523)	(0.251)	(0.341)	(0.148)

Table A.2—Continued

	Army	Air Force	Marine Corps	Navy
Divorced/separated	0.0806***	0.0678	0.104	0.135*
	(0.0212)	(0.0642)	(0.0672)	(0.0605)
Married	0.231***	0.0709***	0.116***	0.224***
	(0.00940)	(0.0164)	(0.0249)	(0.0254)
Widowed	0.408*	1.281	0.755	0.0346
	(0.181)	(0.671)	(0.685)	(0.574)
Number of children	−0.0583***	−0.0591	−0.158**	−0.162***
	(0.00860)	(0.0445)	(0.0606)	(0.0410)
Married with children	−0.240***	−0.323***	−0.211*	−0.386***
	(0.0181)	(0.0606)	(0.0894)	(0.0672)
21–25 years old	−0.0397***	0.00604	0.0505***	−0.00370
	(0.00637)	(0.0102)	(0.0113)	(0.0141)
26–30 years old	0.0123	0.0861***	0.267***	0.0547*
	(0.0112)	(0.0261)	(0.0269)	(0.0266)
31 or older	0.120***	0.0103	0.316*	0.250***
	(0.0160)	(0.359)	(0.147)	(0.0451)
Not a U.S. citizen	−0.208***	−0.342***	−0.164***	−0.221***
	(0.0162)	(0.0401)	(0.0260)	(0.0319)
Prior active-duty service	−0.0110	0.212*	0.285***	−0.112
	(0.0611)	(0.0894)	(0.0604)	(0.0656)
Signed contract during high school	0.0323***	0.00545	−0.0321**	0.0552***
	(0.00843)	(0.0114)	(0.0108)	(0.0152)
Participated in youth program	0.150***	0.0700*	0.0761***	0.0407
	(0.0118)	(0.0344)	(0.0163)	(0.0305)
No DEP	0.0430	−0.119	0.0500	0.128*
	(0.0222)	(0.0726)	(0.0292)	(0.0555)
7–9 months of DEP	−0.0383***	−0.0548***	−0.0481***	−0.0476*
	(0.00880)	(0.0134)	(0.0145)	(0.0198)
10 or more months of DEP	−0.0464***	−0.105***	−0.0647***	−0.0769***
	(0.00732)	(0.0108)	(0.0106)	(0.0137)

Table A.2—Continued

	Army	Air Force	Marine Corps	Navy
Accession rank				
E2	−0.00695	−0.108***	−0.0775***	−0.0665***
	(0.0128)	(0.0158)	(0.0136)	(0.0195)
E3	−0.196***	−0.129***	−0.179***	−0.368***
	(0.00599)	(0.0136)	(0.0106)	(0.0147)
E4 or higher	−0.304***	−0.198***	−1.438***	−0.251***
	(0.00778)	(0.0127)	(0.382)	(0.0158)
DoD occ. category				
Electronics	−0.155***	−0.0621	1.112**	−0.0409
	(0.0123)	(0.180)	(0.374)	(0.159)
COMINT	−0.114***	0.136	0.650	−0.532
	(0.00944)	(0.0741)	(0.564)	(0.346)
Health	−0.162***	−0.699***	—	0.345
	(0.0112)	(0.0790)	—	(0.297)
Other technicians	−0.143***	−0.213*	0.417	—
	(0.0144)	(0.0884)	(0.337)	—
Administrative	−0.176***	−0.632***	0.256	−0.577***
	(0.0107)	(0.0741)	(0.415)	(0.105)
Mechanical	−0.184***	−0.596***	0.630	0.00249
	(0.00927)	(0.0474)	(0.453)	(0.0118)
Craftsworkers	−0.210***	−0.656***	—	−0.195
	(0.0177)	(0.101)	—	(0.278)
Service/supply	−0.0974***	−0.314***	0.296	−1.095**
	(0.00899)	(0.0494)	(0.374)	(0.361)
Non-Occupational	0.112***	0.173***	0.156	—
	(0.00822)	(0.0298)	(0.190)	—
ASVAB percentiles				
Arithmetic reasoning	0.000683**	0.00176***	0.00108**	0.00149***
	(0.000220)	(0.000334)	(0.000328)	(0.000379)
Auto information	−0.000544***	−0.00117***	−0.00118***	−0.000387
	(0.000132)	(0.000195)	(0.000193)	(0.000280)
Coding speed	0.00103***	0.000207	0.00139***	0.000621*
	(0.000128)	(0.000191)	(0.000187)	(0.000261)

Table A.2—Continued

	Army	Air Force	Marine Corps	Navy
Electronics info.	0.000174	−0.000181	0.00202	−0.00135
	(0.000796)	(0.00107)	(0.00114)	(0.00152)
Mathematics	−0.00201***	−0.00191***	−0.00202***	−0.00197***
	(0.000135)	(0.000200)	(0.000201)	(0.000294)
Mechanical comprehension	−0.000880***	−0.000791***	−0.000854***	−0.000820***
	(0.0000947)	(0.000141)	(0.000144)	(0.000193)
Numerical operations	−0.00183***	−0.00177***	−0.00216***	−0.00151***
	(0.000198)	(0.000299)	(0.000292)	(0.000331)
Paragraph comprehension	−0.000322	0.000149	−0.000999*	0.000562
	(0.000326)	(0.000441)	(0.000489)	(0.000656)
Verbal expression	−0.0000827	−0.000269	−0.000432	0.00149*
	(0.000452)	(0.00306)	(0.000649)	(0.000705)
General science	0.000410**	0.000795***	0.000942***	0.000740*
	(0.000139)	(0.000196)	(0.000207)	(0.000296)
Word knowledge	0.00318***	0.00434***	0.00129	0.00397***
	(0.000575)	(0.000772)	(0.000830)	(0.00112)
AFQT percentile	−0.00451***	−0.00930***	−0.00428***	−0.00531***
	(0.000786)	(0.00135)	(0.00117)	(0.00121)
Failed ENTNAC	−0.0415***	−0.00235	0.0200	0.0511*
	(0.00849)	(0.0188)	(0.0140)	(0.0243)
Color vision	−0.0235	0.0828***	−0.0399*	0.00509
	(0.0129)	(0.0239)	(0.0184)	(0.0271)
PULHES: Physical capacity	0.0680***	0.0200	0.128***	0.0624*
	(0.0126)	(0.0237)	(0.0189)	(0.0301)
PULHES: Upper extremities	0.0758**	0.0220	0.0806	−0.0564
	(0.0286)	(0.0531)	(0.0540)	(0.0700)
PULHES: Lower extremities	0.171***	0.131**	0.176***	0.0265
	(0.0244)	(0.0426)	(0.0393)	(0.0556)
PULHES: Hearing	0.0998***	−0.0335	0.142***	0.190***
	(0.0195)	(0.0467)	(0.0351)	(0.0522)

Table A.2—Continued

	Army	Air Force	Marine Corps	Navy
PULHES: Vision	0.0682***	0.0406***	0.0778***	0.0706***
	(0.00589)	(0.00929)	(0.00933)	(0.0125)
PULHES: Psychiatric	−0.0251	0.145***	0.0345	−0.0442
	(0.0285)	(0.0418)	(0.0433)	(0.0724)
BMI	0.00845***	0.0000414	−0.00429***	0.00540**
	(0.000727)	(0.00141)	(0.00130)	(0.00165)
BMI-squared	0.000202**	0.000335**	0.000561***	0.000464**
	(0.0000650)	(0.000111)	(0.000111)	(0.000143)
Constant	−0.749***	−1.041***	−1.217***	−1.111***
	(0.0255)	(0.0585)	(0.194)	(0.0481)
N	546,441	265,254	269,799	141,038
Pseudo-R^2	0.0530	0.0444	0.0410	0.0525

SOURCE: Author calculations from DMDC data merged with BLS data at the county level.

NOTE: Table shows coefficients from probit regressions with three-month attrition as the outcome variable. Standard errors are in parentheses. Statistical significance is denoted by asterisks: * $p < 0.05$, ** $p < 0.01$, *** $p < 0.001$.

Table A.3
Probit Coefficients for 12-Month Attrition Based on Characteristics at Accession

	Army	Air Force	Navy	Marine Corps
County-level unemployment rate	−0.00489***	−0.000210	−0.00440*	−0.00436
	(0.00113)	(0.00184)	(0.00189)	(0.00255)
American Samoa	−0.621***	0.102	−0.282	—
	(0.118)	(0.278)	(0.322)	—
Micronesia	−0.122	—	−0.229	—
	(0.332)	—	(0.178)	—
Marshall Islands	−0.718*	—	—	—
	(0.325)	—	—	—
Mariana Islands	0.696	—	−0.221	—
	(0.553)	—	(0.243)	—
Puerto Rico	−0.0445	−0.0769	0.0565	0.0618
	(0.0276)	(0.0578)	(0.0722)	(0.0660)

Table A.3—Continued

	Army	Air Force	Navy	Marine Corps
Palau	−0.596	—	−0.206	—
	(0.350)	—	(0.456)	—
Minor outlying islands	0.0762	—	—	—
	(0.233)	—	—	—
U.S. Virgin Islands	−0.123	−0.0675	−0.422	−0.199
	(0.0940)	(0.143)	(0.326)	(0.177)
Foreign country	−0.579***	−0.407	−0.307	0.147
	(0.137)	(0.274)	(0.192)	(0.216)
Missing BLS match	0.0103	−0.0875**	−0.0550	−0.0929
	(0.0227)	(0.0310)	(0.0421)	(0.0558)
West	−0.106***	−0.123***	−0.0636***	−0.130***
	(0.00607)	(0.00953)	(0.00995)	(0.0129)
Midwest	−0.0191**	−0.0212*	−0.00983	−0.0175
	(0.00592)	(0.00896)	(0.00933)	(0.0131)
Northeast	−0.0299***	−0.0227*	−0.0147	−0.0617***
	(0.00698)	(0.0110)	(0.0104)	(0.0147)
Accession year				
2003	0.0100	−0.0887***	0.00808	0.149***
	(0.0151)	(0.0205)	(0.0245)	(0.0436)
2004	0.0771***	0.0672***	−0.0783*	0.210***
	(0.0138)	(0.0195)	(0.0362)	(0.0526)
2005	−0.0773***	0.000227	−0.0651**	0.126**
	(0.0146)	(0.0216)	(0.0206)	(0.0419)
2006	−0.287***	0.0526**	−0.0499*	0.134***
	(0.0125)	(0.0194)	(0.0206)	(0.0307)
2007	−0.205***	0.153***	−0.138***	0.233***
	(0.0125)	(0.0195)	(0.0200)	(0.0279)
2008	−0.126***	0.0275	−0.197***	0.133***
	(0.0125)	(0.0202)	(0.0201)	(0.0323)
2009	−0.0771***	−0.130***	−0.154***	0.190***
	(0.0136)	(0.0217)	(0.0227)	(0.0353)
2010	−0.101***	0.0157	−0.220***	−0.0551
	(0.0140)	(0.0240)	(0.0241)	(0.0896)

Table A.3—Continued

	Army	Air Force	Navy	Marine Corps
2011	−0.132***	−0.0273	−0.308***	0.145***
	(0.0140)	(0.0251)	(0.0239)	(0.0302)
2012	−0.120***	−0.111***	−0.324***	0.0982***
	(0.0139)	(0.0253)	(0.0234)	(0.0277)
2013	−0.119***	−0.0345	−0.290***	0.0828**
	(0.0128)	(0.0249)	(0.0226)	(0.0255)
Accession month				
January	−0.0428***	−0.0743***	−0.0798***	−0.227***
	(0.0102)	(0.0173)	(0.0165)	(0.0242)
February	0.0610***	0.000792	0.135***	0.104***
	(0.0109)	(0.0166)	(0.0183)	(0.0228)
March	0.0216	0.00570	0.132***	−0.0295
	(0.0114)	(0.0175)	(0.0182)	(0.0241)
April	−0.0237*	−0.0826***	−0.0230	−0.236***
	(0.0111)	(0.0177)	(0.0195)	(0.0244)
May	0.0226*	0.0296	0.0971***	−0.0138
	(0.0111)	(0.0165)	(0.0174)	(0.0235)
July	−0.0172	−0.0572**	−0.156***	−0.205***
	(0.01000)	(0.0174)	(0.0159)	(0.0211)
August	0.00966	0.00242	0.0348*	−0.0482*
	(0.0100)	(0.0157)	(0.0146)	(0.0211)
September	0.0454***	−0.0178	0.0671***	−0.0731**
	(0.0111)	(0.0177)	(0.0148)	(0.0223)
October	0.107***	−0.0720***	−0.0775***	−0.196***
	(0.0110)	(0.0188)	(0.0185)	(0.0274)
November	0.139***	0.0137	0.109***	0.0589*
	(0.0111)	(0.0167)	(0.0174)	(0.0241)
December	−0.0459	−0.000135	0.127***	−0.113***
	(0.0365)	(0.0184)	(0.0180)	(0.0277)
Female	0.475***	0.178***	0.357***	0.186***
	(0.00654)	(0.00909)	(0.0123)	(0.0122)
Black	−0.195***	−0.138***	−0.0945***	−0.0808***
	(0.00687)	(0.00990)	(0.0121)	(0.0130)

Table A.3—Continued

	Army	Air Force	Navy	Marine Corps
American Indian	−0.0255	0.00882	−0.0233	0.0274
	(0.0181)	(0.0262)	(0.0273)	(0.0153)
Asian	−0.119***	−0.173***	−0.0987***	−0.148***
	(0.0127)	(0.0180)	(0.0209)	(0.0219)
Other nonwhite	−0.0102	−0.138***	−0.0233	−0.0341
	(0.0102)	(0.0372)	(0.0267)	(0.0314)
Hispanic	−0.178***	−0.166***	−0.152***	−0.133***
	(0.00778)	(0.0454)	(0.0129)	(0.0140)
Education				
Less than HS	0.0557***	0.0354	0.178***	0.229***
	(0.0136)	(0.0468)	(0.0529)	(0.0352)
GED or equivalent	0.188***	0.139***	0.129***	0.212***
	(0.00638)	(0.0378)	(0.0152)	(0.0216)
Associate or some college	0.122***	0.0207	0.0815***	0.125***
	(0.00980)	(0.0189)	(0.0243)	(0.0240)
Bachelor's	0.398***	−0.113***	−0.0723	−0.0160
	(0.0270)	(0.0292)	(0.0415)	(0.0304)
Postgraduate	0.453***	−0.406*	−0.374	−0.0652
	(0.0386)	(0.207)	(0.294)	(0.133)
Divorced/separated	0.0891***	0.0556	0.0636	0.141**
	(0.0188)	(0.0590)	(0.0627)	(0.0548)
Married	0.177***	0.0187	0.0752**	0.167***
	(0.00855)	(0.0151)	(0.0231)	(0.0238)
Widowed	0.247	1.145	0.568	0.382
	(0.172)	(0.667)	(0.685)	(0.436)
Number of children	−0.0238**	−0.0433	−0.105*	−0.132***
	(0.00726)	(0.0391)	(0.0516)	(0.0346)
Married with children	−0.204***	−0.263***	−0.145	−0.286***
	(0.0159)	(0.0535)	(0.0767)	(0.0579)
21–25 years old	−0.0508***	−0.0399***	0.0273**	−0.0346**
	(0.00566)	(0.00910)	(0.0102)	(0.0126)
26–30 years old	−0.0364***	0.0439	0.219***	−0.00664
	(0.00983)	(0.0236)	(0.0249)	(0.0242)

Table A.3—Continued

	Army	Air Force	Navy	Marine Corps
31 or older	−0.00323	−0.0180	0.310*	0.158***
	(0.0143)	(0.307)	(0.136)	(0.0417)
Not a U.S. citizen	−0.264***	−0.324***	−0.178***	−0.236***
	(0.0143)	(0.0338)	(0.0233)	(0.0284)
Prior active-duty service	0.0173	0.200*	0.225***	−0.150**
	(0.0519)	(0.0807)	(0.0570)	(0.0578)
Signed contract during high school	−0.00270	0.00321	−0.0231*	0.0387**
	(0.00759)	(0.0101)	(0.00963)	(0.0136)
Participated in youth program	0.161***	0.0722*	0.0543***	0.0310
	(0.0106)	(0.0305)	(0.0146)	(0.0274)
No DEP	0.0117	0.0167	0.0543*	0.145**
	(0.0194)	(0.0603)	(0.0263)	(0.0488)
4–6 months of DEP	−0.0625***	−0.0957***	−0.0748***	−0.0880***
	(0.00610)	(0.00971)	(0.00956)	(0.0128)
7–9 months of DEP	−0.00410	−0.122***	−0.101***	−0.131***
	(0.00863)	(0.0113)	(0.0113)	(0.0139)
10 or more months of DEP	−0.0292**	−0.114***	−0.0917***	−0.118***
	(0.0113)	(0.0141)	(0.0120)	(0.0174)
Accession rank				
E2	−0.199***	−0.130***	−0.156***	−0.295***
	(0.00534)	(0.0120)	(0.00939)	(0.0127)
E3	−0.325***	−0.207***	−1.093***	−0.237***
	(0.00691)	(0.0113)	(0.246)	(0.0142)
E4 or higher	−0.123***	−0.423	−0.914***	−0.181
	(0.0264)	(0.405)	(0.224)	(0.153)
DoD occ. category				
Electronics	−0.0959***	−0.158	1.022**	0.162
	(0.0108)	(0.157)	(0.325)	(0.124)
COMINT	−0.0921***	0.155*	0.761	−0.646*
	(0.00847)	(0.0622)	(0.444)	(0.287)
Health	−0.0676***	−0.524***	—	0.637*
	(0.00976)	(0.0569)	—	(0.253)

Table A.3—Continued

	Army	Air Force	Navy	Marine Corps
Other technicians	−0.0859***	−0.133	0.611*	—
	(0.0127)	(0.0703)	(0.293)	—
Administrative	−0.181***	−0.539***	0.511	−0.462***
	(0.00973)	(0.0560)	(0.305)	(0.0825)
Mechanical	−0.132***	−0.513***	0.553	0.0123
	(0.00831)	(0.0372)	(0.361)	(0.0107)
Craftsworkers	−0.141***	−0.452***	0.824	−0.290
	(0.0156)	(0.0707)	(0.632)	(0.264)
Service/supply	−0.0883***	−0.260***	0.268	−0.325
	(0.00817)	(0.0396)	(0.318)	(0.171)
Non-Occupational	0.243***	0.0801**	0.263	—
	(0.00717)	(0.0256)	(0.166)	—
ASVAB percentiles				
Arithmetic reasoning	0.00138***	0.00136***	0.000819**	0.00169***
	(0.000196)	(0.000298)	(0.000292)	(0.000336)
Auto information	−0.000682***	−0.00158***	−0.00108***	−0.000556*
	(0.000117)	(0.000172)	(0.000171)	(0.000252)
Coding speed	0.00105***	−0.0000110	0.00113***	0.000353
	(0.000113)	(0.000169)	(0.000168)	(0.000233)
Electronics info.	−0.0000454	0.000386	0.00134	−0.0000737
	(0.000705)	(0.000956)	(0.00102)	(0.00135)
Mathematics	−0.00208***	−0.00165***	−0.00201***	−0.00173***
	(0.000119)	(0.000178)	(0.000179)	(0.000265)
Mechanical comprehension	−0.000831***	−0.000629***	−0.000781***	−0.000652***
	(0.0000838)	(0.000125)	(0.000129)	(0.000171)
Num. operations	−0.00140***	−0.00224***	−0.00251***	−0.00165***
	(0.000176)	(0.000266)	(0.000260)	(0.000294)
Paragraph comprehension	0.000225	−0.000587	−0.000599	0.000142
	(0.000287)	(0.000395)	(0.000437)	(0.000586)
Verbal expression	0.000722	−0.00233	−0.000621	0.00101
	(0.000407)	(0.00271)	(0.000580)	(0.000618)
General science	0.000306*	0.000556**	0.000787***	0.000377
	(0.000123)	(0.000174)	(0.000185)	(0.000267)

Table A.3—Continued

	Army	Air Force	Navy	Marine Corps
Word knowledge	0.00378***	0.00327***	0.00158*	0.00306**
	(0.000508)	(0.000694)	(0.000741)	(0.00101)
AFQT percentile	−0.00501***	−0.00670***	−0.00380***	−0.00460***
	(0.000701)	(0.00121)	(0.00104)	(0.00104)
Failed ENTNAC	−0.0205**	0.0549***	0.0401**	0.117***
	(0.00734)	(0.0165)	(0.0126)	(0.0207)
Color vision	−0.0172	0.102***	−0.0335*	0.00155
	(0.0114)	(0.0214)	(0.0165)	(0.0240)
PULHES: Physical capacity	0.0565***	0.00400	0.0982***	0.0128
	(0.0112)	(0.0212)	(0.0173)	(0.0278)
PULHES: Upper extremities	0.0319	−0.00172	0.0278	−0.0722
	(0.0256)	(0.0482)	(0.0503)	(0.0634)
PULHES: Lower extremities	0.129***	0.112**	0.137***	0.0191
	(0.0222)	(0.0388)	(0.0364)	(0.0503)
PULHES: Hearing	0.0796***	−0.0460	0.0962**	0.148**
	(0.0176)	(0.0419)	(0.0323)	(0.0480)
PULHES: Vision	0.0576***	0.0196*	0.0670***	0.0430***
	(0.00522)	(0.00836)	(0.00841)	(0.0114)
PULHES: Psychiatric	−0.0136	0.0980*	−0.0171	−0.0556
	(0.0253)	(0.0384)	(0.0400)	(0.0654)
BMI	0.00640***	−0.00451***	−0.0114***	−0.0000410
	(0.000647)	(0.00125)	(0.00115)	(0.00147)
BMI-squared	0.000238***	0.000359***	0.000648***	0.000414**
	(0.0000694)	(0.000106)	(0.000116)	(0.000134)
Constant	−0.617***	−0.743***	−1.049***	−0.806***
	(0.0227)	(0.0519)	(0.169)	(0.0428)
N	546441	265254	269811	141038
Pseudo-R^2	0.0546	0.0381	0.0387	0.0400

SOURCE: Author calculations from DMDC data merged with BLS data at the county level.

NOTE: Table shows coefficients from probit regressions with three-month attrition as the outcome variable. Standard errors are in parentheses. Statistical significance is denoted by asterisks: * $p < 0.05$, ** $p < 0.01$, *** $p < 0.001$.

Table A.4
Probit Coefficients for 36-Month Attrition Based on Characteristics at Accession

	Army	Air Force	Marine Corps	Navy
County-level unemployment rate	−0.00236*	−0.000742	−0.00453**	−0.00204
	(0.000949)	(0.00151)	(0.00156)	(0.00211)
American Samoa	−0.449***	−0.197	−0.617	−0.0167
	(0.0870)	(0.243)	(0.321)	(0.362)
Micronesia	−0.273	0.860	−0.294	—
	(0.290)	(0.585)	(0.152)	—
Marshall Islands	−0.868**	—	—	—
	(0.266)	—	—	—
Mariana Islands	0.144	—	−0.0726	—
	(0.546)	—	(0.188)	—
Puerto Rico	−0.150***	−0.149**	0.0297	−0.0997
	(0.0232)	(0.0486)	(0.0622)	(0.0569)
Palau	−0.834*	—	−0.458	—
	(0.325)	—	(0.462)	—
Minor outlying islands	0.352	—	—	—
	(0.216)	—	—	—
U.S. Virgin Islands	−0.313***	−0.231*	−0.480	−0.283
	(0.0805)	(0.117)	(0.255)	(0.147)
Foreign country	−0.239*	−0.255	−0.130	−0.104
	(0.0981)	(0.180)	(0.151)	(0.195)
Missing BLS match	−0.0263	−0.0285	−0.126***	−0.0876
	(0.0195)	(0.0254)	(0.0359)	(0.0456)
West	−0.123***	−0.109***	−0.0778***	−0.141***
	(0.00513)	(0.00777)	(0.00831)	(0.0106)
Midwest	−0.0362***	−0.0212**	−0.0327***	−0.0230*
	(0.00505)	(0.00744)	(0.00787)	(0.0110)
Northeast	−0.0262***	−0.0191*	−0.0122	−0.0479***
	(0.00593)	(0.00909)	(0.00876)	(0.0122)
Accession year				
2003	0.00599	−0.0305	−0.0208	0.161***
	(0.0130)	(0.0165)	(0.0211)	(0.0349)

Table A.4—Continued

	Army	Air Force	Marine Corps	Navy
2004	−0.0371**	−0.0530**	−0.0588	0.266***
	(0.0121)	(0.0161)	(0.0307)	(0.0431)
2005	−0.174***	−0.121***	−0.0596***	0.173***
	(0.0127)	(0.0178)	(0.0175)	(0.0342)
2006	−0.270***	−0.128***	−0.0906***	0.148***
	(0.0107)	(0.0161)	(0.0176)	(0.0247)
2007	−0.177***	−0.0876***	−0.128***	0.0985***
	(0.0107)	(0.0163)	(0.0170)	(0.0230)
2008	−0.154***	−0.104***	−0.132***	0.0510
	(0.0107)	(0.0166)	(0.0170)	(0.0265)
2009	−0.141***	−0.156***	−0.138***	0.115***
	(0.0117)	(0.0176)	(0.0192)	(0.0285)
2010	−0.128***	−0.109***	−0.170***	−0.0357
	(0.0120)	(0.0197)	(0.0202)	(0.0694)
2011	−0.122***	−0.171***	−0.237***	0.0205
	(0.0119)	(0.0206)	(0.0199)	(0.0246)
2012	−0.123***	−0.202***	−0.257***	−0.0781***
	(0.0119)	(0.0205)	(0.0196)	(0.0226)
2013	−0.135***	−0.237***	−0.235***	−0.0759***
	(0.0110)	(0.0205)	(0.0189)	(0.0208)
Accession month				
January	−0.0153	−0.0263	−0.0451***	−0.103***
	(0.00857)	(0.0142)	(0.0136)	(0.0198)
February	0.0397***	−0.00408	0.0961***	0.0844***
	(0.00925)	(0.0140)	(0.0156)	(0.0198)
March	0.0408***	0.0201	0.0922***	0.00693
	(0.00960)	(0.0148)	(0.0155)	(0.0207)
April	−0.00667	−0.0451**	0.000804	−0.0981***
	(0.00937)	(0.0145)	(0.0162)	(0.0200)
May	0.00959	0.0198	0.0697***	0.0133
	(0.00939)	(0.0139)	(0.0147)	(0.0202)
July	−0.00787	−0.0197	−0.0722***	−0.116***
	(0.00839)	(0.0143)	(0.0127)	(0.0177)

Table A.4—Continued

	Army	Air Force	Marine Corps	Navy
August	0.00217	−0.000716	0.0288*	−0.0352
	(0.00847)	(0.0132)	(0.0121)	(0.0181)
September	0.0226*	−0.0271	0.0212	−0.0581**
	(0.00941)	(0.0150)	(0.0124)	(0.0192)
October	0.0600***	0.00216	−0.0315*	−0.0635**
	(0.00939)	(0.0153)	(0.0151)	(0.0226)
November	0.0893***	0.0455**	0.0923***	0.0421*
	(0.00952)	(0.0140)	(0.0147)	(0.0208)
December	0.139***	0.0223	0.0926***	−0.0718**
	(0.0300)	(0.0155)	(0.0153)	(0.0235)
Female	0.501***	0.160***	0.297***	0.102***
	(0.00569)	(0.00762)	(0.0109)	(0.0103)
Black	−0.129***	−0.0347***	−0.0453***	−0.0498***
	(0.00570)	(0.00797)	(0.0101)	(0.0108)
American Indian	0.0149	0.0477*	0.00690	0.0605***
	(0.0155)	(0.0211)	(0.0227)	(0.0128)
Asian	−0.145***	−0.165***	−0.134***	−0.149***
	(0.0106)	(0.0144)	(0.0175)	(0.0178)
Other nonwhite	−0.0248**	−0.132***	−0.00703	−0.0381
	(0.00877)	(0.0305)	(0.0227)	(0.0258)
Hispanic	−0.189***	−0.172***	−0.177***	−0.133***
	(0.00642)	(0.0353)	(0.0106)	(0.0115)
Education				
Less than high school	0.0811***	0.0676	0.149**	0.320***
	(0.0114)	(0.0382)	(0.0461)	(0.0296)
GED or equivalent	0.242***	0.198***	0.195***	0.286***
	(0.00552)	(0.0315)	(0.0130)	(0.0183)
Associate or some college	0.109***	−0.00912	0.132***	0.147***
	(0.00824)	(0.0156)	(0.0207)	(0.0201)
Bachelor's	0.176***	−0.0274	0.0234	−0.0305
	(0.0234)	(0.0227)	(0.0339)	(0.0255)
Postgraduate	0.344***	−0.188	−0.0722	−0.107
	(0.0352)	(0.141)	(0.219)	(0.116)

Table A.4—Continued

	Army	Air Force	Marine Corps	Navy
Divorced/separated	0.114***	0.129**	0.0783	0.154**
	(0.0166)	(0.0491)	(0.0552)	(0.0471)
Married	0.103***	−0.0674***	0.0223	0.0880***
	(0.00760)	(0.0128)	(0.0204)	(0.0209)
Widowed	0.284	0.820	0.223	0.0315
	(0.160)	(0.645)	(0.687)	(0.440)
Number of children	−0.00544	−0.0276	−0.0615	−0.0448
	(0.00612)	(0.0298)	(0.0431)	(0.0258)
Married with children	−0.138***	−0.146***	−0.139*	−0.197***
	(0.0136)	(0.0414)	(0.0648)	(0.0454)
21–25 years old	−0.103***	−0.112***	−0.0299***	−0.0833***
	(0.00478)	(0.00751)	(0.00869)	(0.0105)
26–30 years old	−0.123***	−0.105***	0.117***	−0.102***
	(0.00847)	(0.0197)	(0.0221)	(0.0203)
31 or older	−0.111***	−0.0439	0.222	−0.00149
	(0.0124)	(0.224)	(0.125)	(0.0362)
Not a U.S. citizen	−0.208***	−0.316***	−0.204***	−0.316***
	(0.0113)	(0.0257)	(0.0193)	(0.0230)
Prior active-duty service	−0.00465	0.135	0.0836	−0.104*
	(0.0449)	(0.0700)	(0.0532)	(0.0455)
Signed contract during high school	−0.0255***	0.00627	0.00862	0.0236*
	(0.00633)	(0.00830)	(0.00799)	(0.0113)
Participated in youth program	0.121***	0.0383	0.0579***	0.0143
	(0.00889)	(0.0252)	(0.0121)	(0.0224)
No DEP	0.0106	0.00929	0.0613**	0.0963*
	(0.0166)	(0.0496)	(0.0228)	(0.0421)
4–6 months of DEP	−0.0333***	−0.0922***	−0.0904***	−0.0851***
	(0.00663)	(0.00994)	(0.0111)	(0.0147)
7–9 months of DEP	−0.0457***	−0.154***	−0.131***	−0.145***
	(0.00551)	(0.00803)	(0.00799)	(0.0102)
10 or more months of DEP	−0.0459***	−0.183***	−0.124***	−0.155***
	(0.00952)	(0.0117)	(0.0100)	(0.0143)

Table A.4—Continued

	Army	Air Force	Marine Corps	Navy
Accession rank				
E2	−0.178***	−0.143***	−0.149***	−0.233***
	(0.00447)	(0.00982)	(0.00777)	(0.0102)
E3	−0.288***	−0.187***	0.0337	−0.203***
	(0.00565)	(0.00907)	(0.122)	(0.0116)
E4 or higher	−0.0638**	−0.0727	0.164	−0.0695
	(0.0227)	(0.218)	(0.127)	(0.111)
DoD occupational category				
Electronics	−0.109***	0.0136	0.326	0.262*
	(0.00902)	(0.111)	(0.267)	(0.110)
COMINT	−0.115***	0.00241	0.0958	0.0198
	(0.00708)	(0.0518)	(0.312)	(0.178)
Health	−0.102***	−0.289***	—	0.681**
	(0.00826)	(0.0396)	—	(0.238)
Other technicians	−0.116***	−0.0911	−0.258	−1.012*
	(0.0107)	(0.0525)	(0.230)	(0.494)
Administrative	−0.168***	−0.296***	0.375*	−0.198***
	(0.00810)	(0.0374)	(0.184)	(0.0551)
Mechanical	−0.127***	−0.281***	0.0738	0.0490***
	(0.00691)	(0.0265)	(0.208)	(0.00887)
Craftsworkers	−0.0696***	−0.340***	0.433	−0.162
	(0.0127)	(0.0488)	(0.384)	(0.192)
Service/supply	−0.0382***	−0.0857**	0.608**	−0.147
	(0.00681)	(0.0293)	(0.190)	(0.118)
Non-Occupational	0.139***	−0.00861	−0.521***	−0.0670
	(0.00634)	(0.0205)	(0.0954)	(0.646)
ASVAB percentiles				
Arithmetic reasoning	0.000616***	0.000586*	0.000451	0.00205***
	(0.000167)	(0.000244)	(0.000245)	(0.000277)
Auto information	−0.00117***	−0.00167***	−0.00102***	−0.00111***
	(0.0000982)	(0.000142)	(0.000143)	(0.000210)
Coding speed	0.000527***	−0.000447**	0.000665***	0.000208
	(0.0000956)	(0.000139)	(0.000141)	(0.000192)

Table A.4—Continued

	Army	Air Force	Marine Corps	Navy
Electronics information	−0.000639	0.000788	0.000953	0.00180
	(0.000597)	(0.000789)	(0.000861)	(0.00112)
Mathematics	−0.00178***	−0.00143***	−0.00179***	−0.00170***
	(0.000101)	(0.000146)	(0.000150)	(0.000221)
Mechanical Comprehension	−0.000838***	−0.000435***	−0.000736***	−0.000507***
	(0.0000709)	(0.000103)	(0.000108)	(0.000140)
Numerical operations	−0.00216***	−0.00247***	−0.00282***	−0.00139***
	(0.000150)	(0.000218)	(0.000219)	(0.000243)
Paragraph comprehension	−0.000148	−0.00100**	−0.000572	−0.000409
	(0.000243)	(0.000325)	(0.000367)	(0.000485)
Verbal expression	−0.000804*	0.00167	−0.00112*	0.00155**
	(0.000356)	(0.00156)	(0.000496)	(0.000509)
General science	0.000199	0.000375**	0.000484**	0.000137
	(0.000104)	(0.000144)	(0.000155)	(0.000223)
Word knowledge	0.00288***	0.00234***	0.00110	0.00223**
	(0.000430)	(0.000570)	(0.000625)	(0.000836)
AFQT percentile	−0.00157**	−0.00404***	−0.00219*	−0.00612***
	(0.000602)	(0.000995)	(0.000875)	(0.000847)
Failed ENTNAC	0.0822***	0.142***	0.132***	0.239***
	(0.00620)	(0.0134)	(0.0107)	(0.0169)
Color vision	−0.0271**	0.0644***	−0.0208	0.0247
	(0.00963)	(0.0170)	(0.0139)	(0.0198)
PULHES: Physical capacity	−0.00519	−0.0258	0.0529***	−0.00319
	(0.00983)	(0.0178)	(0.0151)	(0.0234)
PULHES: Upper extremities	−0.0169	−0.0429	−0.0236	−0.0807
	(0.0221)	(0.0401)	(0.0437)	(0.0521)
PULHES: Lower extremities	0.0698***	0.0149	0.101**	−0.000963
	(0.0196)	(0.0336)	(0.0319)	(0.0425)
PULHES: Hearing	0.0530***	−0.00218	0.0461	0.0994*
	(0.0153)	(0.0340)	(0.0280)	(0.0412)

Table A.4—Continued

	Army	Air Force	Marine Corps	Navy
PULHES: Vision	0.0256***	−0.000302	0.0287***	0.0117
	(0.00448)	(0.00696)	(0.00717)	(0.00958)
PULHES: Psychiatric	0.0110	0.112***	−0.00742	0.00198
	(0.0215)	(0.0323)	(0.0340)	(0.0530)
BMI	0.00975***	0.00114	−0.00674***	0.00179
	(0.000591)	(0.00105)	(0.000957)	(0.00122)
BMI-squared	0.000298**	0.000434***	0.000521***	0.000733**
	(0.000105)	(0.000125)	(0.000116)	(0.000230)
Constant	−0.0224	−0.0823	0.129	−0.234***
	(0.0193)	(0.0423)	(0.0994)	(0.0356)
N	546441	265285	269811	141085
Pseudo-R^2	0.0443	0.0330	0.0308	0.0397

SOURCE: Author calculations from DMDC data merged with BLS data at the county level.

NOTE: Table shows coefficients from probit regressions with three-month attrition as the outcome variable. Standard errors are in parentheses. Statistical significance is denoted by asterisks: * $p < 0.05$, ** $p < 0.01$, *** $p < 0.001$.

Table A.5
Probit Coefficients for 7-to-36-Month Attrition Based on Characteristics at Accession

	Army	Air Force	Navy	Marine Corps
County-level unemployment rate	−0.000255	−0.00124	−0.00540**	−0.00129
	(0.00105)	(0.00168)	(0.00178)	(0.00240)
American Samoa	−0.326***	−0.0810	—	0.278
	(0.0943)	(0.258)	—	(0.355)
Micronesia	−0.139	1.134*	−0.306	—
	(0.308)	(0.564)	(0.187)	—
Marshall Islands	−0.872*	—	—	—
	(0.342)	—	—	—
Mariana Islands	—	—	0.00977	—
	—	—	(0.214)	—
Puerto Rico	−0.150***	−0.162**	0.00806	−0.217**
	(0.0255)	(0.0559)	(0.0728)	(0.0682)

Table A.5—Continued

	Army	Air Force	Navy	Marine Corps
Palau	−0.997*	—	—	—
	(0.479)	—	—	—
Minor outlying islands	0.339	—	—	—
	(0.253)	—	—	—
U.S. Virgin Islands	−0.322***	−0.270*	−0.553	−0.307
	(0.0926)	(0.132)	(0.314)	(0.171)
Foreign country	−0.104	−0.167	0.0600	−0.274
	(0.104)	(0.190)	(0.159)	(0.237)
Missing BLS match	−0.0461*	−0.000763	−0.159***	−0.0794
	(0.0219)	(0.0280)	(0.0419)	(0.0518)
West	−0.119***	−0.0770***	−0.0655***	−0.112***
	(0.00566)	(0.00865)	(0.00946)	(0.0120)
Midwest	−0.0517***	−0.0251**	−0.0353***	−0.0122
	(0.00562)	(0.00837)	(0.00902)	(0.0125)
Northeast	−0.0279***	−0.0181	−0.00938	−0.0237
	(0.00655)	(0.0102)	(0.0100)	(0.0139)
Accession year				
2003	0.0145	−0.0213	−0.0475	0.153***
	(0.0145)	(0.0183)	(0.0243)	(0.0380)
2004	−0.0959***	−0.0982***	−0.0712*	0.233***
	(0.0136)	(0.0180)	(0.0352)	(0.0468)
2005	−0.175***	−0.163***	−0.0655**	0.163***
	(0.0142)	(0.0200)	(0.0200)	(0.0373)
2006	−0.136***	−0.219***	−0.124***	0.124***
	(0.0117)	(0.0181)	(0.0202)	(0.0270)
2007	−0.0760***	−0.257***	−0.141***	−0.0195
	(0.0118)	(0.0186)	(0.0194)	(0.0257)
2008	−0.0935***	−0.180***	−0.109***	−0.0453
	(0.0119)	(0.0187)	(0.0194)	(0.0296)
2009	−0.125***	−0.148***	−0.140***	0.0280
	(0.0131)	(0.0195)	(0.0219)	(0.0317)
2010	−0.111***	−0.145***	−0.148***	−0.0496
	(0.0133)	(0.0220)	(0.0231)	(0.0758)

Table A.5—Continued

	Army	Air Force	Navy	Marine Corps
2011	−0.0896***	−0.217***	−0.184***	−0.115***
	(0.0132)	(0.0231)	(0.0226)	(0.0275)
2012	−0.144***	−0.223***	−0.182***	−0.221***
	(0.0133)	(0.0228)	(0.0222)	(0.0252)
2013	−0.139***	−0.317***	−0.190***	−0.207***
	(0.0123)	(0.0231)	(0.0216)	(0.0232)
Accession month				
January	−0.0311***	−0.0194	−0.00213	0.0106
	(0.00942)	(0.0159)	(0.0154)	(0.0226)
February	0.00329	−0.0228	0.0444*	0.0229
	(0.0102)	(0.0159)	(0.0182)	(0.0235)
March	0.0384***	0.0223	0.0661***	0.0196
	(0.0105)	(0.0167)	(0.0178)	(0.0241)
April	−0.0169	−0.0305	0.0311	0.0275
	(0.0103)	(0.0163)	(0.0183)	(0.0227)
May	−0.0153	−0.0157	0.0208	0.0188
	(0.0104)	(0.0158)	(0.0171)	(0.0235)
July	0.0163	−0.0106	−0.00451	−0.0110
	(0.00917)	(0.0160)	(0.0142)	(0.0203)
August	0.00927	−0.00948	0.0277*	−0.0112
	(0.00928)	(0.0150)	(0.0138)	(0.0211)
September	0.0377***	−0.00525	−0.00508	−0.0253
	(0.0103)	(0.0168)	(0.0142)	(0.0225)
October	0.0208*	0.0246	0.0183	0.0488
	(0.0104)	(0.0169)	(0.0171)	(0.0256)
November	0.0413***	0.0363*	0.0653***	0.0169
	(0.0105)	(0.0158)	(0.0169)	(0.0244)
December	0.205***	0.0410*	0.0541**	−0.00226
	(0.0321)	(0.0174)	(0.0177)	(0.0271)
Female	0.443***	0.116***	0.175***	0.00515
	(0.00627)	(0.00859)	(0.0128)	(0.0120)
Black	−0.0807***	0.0296***	−0.0392***	−0.0350**
	(0.00628)	(0.00877)	(0.0116)	(0.0123)

Table A.5—Continued

	Army	Air Force	Navy	Marine Corps
American Indian	0.0274	0.0500*	0.00642	0.0605***
	(0.0171)	(0.0233)	(0.0260)	(0.0146)
Asian	−0.127***	−0.131***	−0.148***	−0.142***
	(0.0117)	(0.0160)	(0.0203)	(0.0203)
Other nonwhite	−0.0203*	−0.113**	0.0135	−0.0319
	(0.00963)	(0.0343)	(0.0257)	(0.0288)
Hispanic	−0.155***	−0.165***	−0.155***	−0.101***
	(0.00705)	(0.0387)	(0.0120)	(0.0130)
Education				
Less than high school	0.0829***	0.0536	0.133*	0.331***
	(0.0124)	(0.0425)	(0.0528)	(0.0319)
GED or equivalent	0.235***	0.204***	0.203***	0.282***
	(0.00608)	(0.0350)	(0.0147)	(0.0202)
Associate or some college	0.0874***	−0.0268	0.144***	0.145***
	(0.00921)	(0.0178)	(0.0238)	(0.0227)
Bachelor's	0.173***	0.0454	0.0923*	−0.0156
	(0.0249)	(0.0249)	(0.0384)	(0.0297)
Postgraduate	0.358***	−0.0612	0.145	−0.0434
	(0.0373)	(0.148)	(0.237)	(0.139)
Divorced/separated	0.108***	0.135*	0.0369	0.140**
	(0.0185)	(0.0557)	(0.0660)	(0.0539)
Married	0.0127	−0.138***	−0.0533*	−0.0352
	(0.00870)	(0.0151)	(0.0248)	(0.0256)
Widowed	0.164	—	—	−0.00955
	(0.191)	—	—	(0.540)
Number of children	0.0182**	−0.00448	0.00463	0.00910
	(0.00664)	(0.0326)	(0.0482)	(0.0278)
Married with children	−0.0501***	−0.0263	−0.0443	−0.0303
	(0.0151)	(0.0457)	(0.0733)	(0.0507)
21–25 years old	−0.113***	−0.153***	−0.0755***	−0.111***
	(0.00530)	(0.00849)	(0.0101)	(0.0119)
26–30 years old	−0.163***	−0.193***	−0.0146	−0.172***
	(0.00944)	(0.0228)	(0.0268)	(0.0236)

Table A.5—Continued

	Army	Air Force	Navy	Marine Corps
31 or older	−0.198***	−0.0794	0.0926	−0.150***
	(0.0140)	(0.236)	(0.147)	(0.0435)
Not a U.S. citizen	−0.171***	−0.255***	−0.190***	−0.317***
	(0.0123)	(0.0280)	(0.0222)	(0.0263)
Prior active-duty service	0.0100	0.0634	−0.0942	−0.0703
	(0.0493)	(0.0805)	(0.0682)	(0.0501)
Signed contract during high school	−0.0528***	0.00623	0.0286**	0.00276
	(0.00708)	(0.00930)	(0.00913)	(0.0128)
Participated in youth program	0.0858***	0.0140	0.0362**	0.00128
	(0.00987)	(0.0281)	(0.0138)	(0.0254)
No DEP	−0.00569	0.0621	0.0576*	0.0651
	(0.0182)	(0.0536)	(0.0262)	(0.0471)
4–6 months of DEP	−0.0386***	−0.127***	−0.122***	−0.112***
	(0.00573)	(0.00899)	(0.00934)	(0.0120)
7–9 months of DEP	−0.00904	−0.157***	−0.146***	−0.177***
	(0.00816)	(0.0105)	(0.0108)	(0.0133)
10 or more months of DEP	−0.0495***	−0.184***	−0.126***	−0.172***
	(0.0106)	(0.0132)	(0.0114)	(0.0162)
Accession rank				
E2	−0.135***	−0.122***	−0.103***	−0.122***
	(0.00494)	(0.0110)	(0.00883)	(0.0113)
E3	−0.227***	−0.147***	0.292*	−0.135***
	(0.00624)	(0.0101)	(0.123)	(0.0132)
E4 or higher	0.0580*	−0.0281	0.447***	−0.000103
	(0.0241)	(0.227)	(0.129)	(0.115)
DoD occ. category				
Electronics	−0.0668***	0.0417	0.119	0.328**
	(0.00993)	(0.118)	(0.297)	(0.117)
COMINT	−0.0924***	−0.0576	−0.0199	0.160
	(0.00787)	(0.0573)	(0.319)	(0.182)
Health	−0.0549***	−0.136***	—	0.710**
	(0.00909)	(0.0411)	—	(0.263)

Table A.5—Continued

	Army	Air Force	Navy	Marine Corps
Other technicians	−0.0812***	−0.0465	−0.437	−0.788
	(0.0118)	(0.0555)	(0.254)	(0.485)
Administrative	−0.129***	−0.185***	0.348	−0.0324
	(0.00900)	(0.0390)	(0.187)	(0.0573)
Mechanical	−0.0756***	−0.169***	−0.0731	0.0674***
	(0.00766)	(0.0281)	(0.213)	(0.0101)
Craftsworkers	0.00480	−0.236***	0.438	−0.111
	(0.0139)	(0.0506)	(0.374)	(0.212)
Service/supply	−0.00326	−0.0287	0.590**	0.0472
	(0.00755)	(0.0310)	(0.194)	(0.119)
Non-Occupational	0.127***	−0.101***	−0.639***	0.0621
	(0.00703)	(0.0224)	(0.0963)	(0.657)
ASVAB percentiles				
Arithmetic reasoning	0.000427*	−0.000112	−0.0000179	0.00210***
	(0.000185)	(0.000274)	(0.000279)	(0.000312)
Auto information	−0.00122***	−0.00161***	−0.000711***	−0.00132***
	(0.000109)	(0.000159)	(0.000162)	(0.000240)
Coding speed	0.000182	−0.000689***	0.000109	−0.0000328
	(0.000106)	(0.000156)	(0.000161)	(0.000217)
Electronics info.	−0.000924	0.00114	0.0000661	0.00309*
	(0.000662)	(0.000887)	(0.000983)	(0.00127)
Mathematics	−0.00135***	−0.000930***	−0.00131***	−0.00121***
	(0.000111)	(0.000164)	(0.000171)	(0.000253)
Mechanical comprehension	−0.000650***	−0.000165	−0.000520***	−0.000251
	(0.0000784)	(0.000115)	(0.000123)	(0.000157)
Numerical operations	−0.00194***	−0.00237***	−0.00264***	−0.000961***
	(0.000166)	(0.000245)	(0.000250)	(0.000274)
Paragraph comprehension	−0.0000577	−0.00141***	−0.000175	−0.000745
	(0.000269)	(0.000365)	(0.000420)	(0.000549)
Verbal expression	−0.00109**	0.000686	−0.00138*	0.00147**
	(0.000401)	(0.00160)	(0.000569)	(0.000567)
General science	0.0000578	0.0000875	0.000120	−0.000196
	(0.000114)	(0.000160)	(0.000177)	(0.000255)

Table A.5—Continued

	Army	Air Force	Navy	Marine Corps
Word knowledge	0.00216***	0.000884	0.000794	0.000978
	(0.000477)	(0.000642)	(0.000714)	(0.000951)
AFQT percentile	0.000284	−0.000632	−0.000484	−0.00578***
	(0.000671)	(0.00112)	(0.000998)	(0.000932)
Failed ENTNAC	0.118***	0.186***	0.171***	0.269***
	(0.00673)	(0.0147)	(0.0121)	(0.0182)
Color vision	−0.0241*	0.0459*	−0.00523	0.0331
	(0.0107)	(0.0189)	(0.0159)	(0.0223)
PULHES: Physical capacity	−0.0402***	−0.0436*	−0.00985	−0.0433
	(0.0111)	(0.0202)	(0.0179)	(0.0273)
PULHES: Upper extremities	−0.0565*	−0.0699	−0.0914	−0.0802
	(0.0250)	(0.0458)	(0.0526)	(0.0596)
PULHES: Lower extremities	0.00282	−0.0577	0.0261	−0.0147
	(0.0224)	(0.0392)	(0.0380)	(0.0488)
PULHES: Hearing	0.0169	0.0145	−0.0294	0.0184
	(0.0173)	(0.0379)	(0.0332)	(0.0474)
PULHES: Vision	0.00162	−0.0225**	−0.00774	−0.0256*
	(0.00498)	(0.00786)	(0.00830)	(0.0111)
PULHES: Psychiatric	0.0277	0.0700	−0.0322	0.0332
	(0.0238)	(0.0369)	(0.0399)	(0.0598)
BMI	0.00892***	0.00140	−0.00692***	−0.000327
	(0.000611)	(0.00117)	(0.00110)	(0.00138)
BMI-squared	0.000194*	0.000354**	0.000307***	0.000596**
	(0.0000759)	(0.000117)	(0.0000821)	(0.000183)
Constant	−0.385***	−0.301***	−0.0629	−0.494***
	(0.0214)	(0.0471)	(0.101)	(0.0403)
N	495,258	246,846	252,535	130,966
Pseudo-R^2	0.0358	0.0284	0.0224	0.0415

SOURCE: Author calculations from DMDC data merged with BLS data at the county level.

NOTE: Table shows coefficients from probit regressions with three-month attrition as the outcome variable. Standard errors are in parentheses. Statistical significance is denoted by asterisks: * $p < 0.05$, ** $p < 0.01$, *** $p < 0.001$.

Robustness Checks

One concern about the sample is that those who enlisted in FY 2002 are different from those who enlisted later. In particular, the terrorist attacks of September 11, 2001, may have affected people's reasons for enlisting (or not enlisting), making the FY 2002 cohort different from later cohorts. Table B.1 shows that FY 2002 enlistees attrite at higher rates than others, almost uniformly across the services. At the three- and six-month marks, FY 2002 enlistees attrite at higher rates in the

Table B.1
Attrition Among Accessions in FY 2002 Versus FYs 2003–2013

Variable	Army		Air Force		Navy		Marine Corps	
	FY 2002	FYs 2003–2013	FY 2002	FYs 2003–2013	FY 2002	FYs 2003–2013	FY 2002	FYs 2003–2013
Number of accessions	77,179	794,247	37,209	320,542	43,920	394,987	32,140	349,229
Attrition rates (percentage)								
3-month attrition	6.9	4.9	4.4	5.1	6.1	6.3	7.1	5.1
6-month attrition	12.4	9.6	9.4	9.0	8.1	8.5	9.9	7.5
12-month attrition	17.7	14.7	13.1	12.1	12.4	11.7	13.8	10.2
36-month attrition	34.6	29.3	26.7	22.7	26.8	23.2	22.6	18.1

SOURCE: Author's calculation from DMDC data merged with BLS data at the county level.

83

Army and Marine Corps. At the 12- and 36-month marks, FY 2002 enlistees in every service have attrition rates 1 to 4 percentage points higher than later enlistees.

Figure B.1 shows that the marginal effects of various characteristics are unchanged after excluding FY 2002 enlistees. For space considerations, the figure shows only the marginal effects for Army recruits. Both the qualitative patterns and the magnitudes of the effects reflect those of the figures in Chapter Four. The statistical significance is also generally the same, although the marginal effect of zero DEP is not statistically significant for any attrition threshold. Comparable figures for other services, although not shown here, also show similar patterns to the figures in Chapter Four.

Table B.2 and Figure B.2 show corresponding attrition and marginal effects for the set of enlistees in FY 2008 or later. This demonstrates whether the results are sensitive to the exclusion of all enlistees from the first part of the Global War on Terror. The results are similar

Figure B.1
Marginal Effects of Accession Characteristics on Attrition for Army Enlistees in FYs 2003–2013

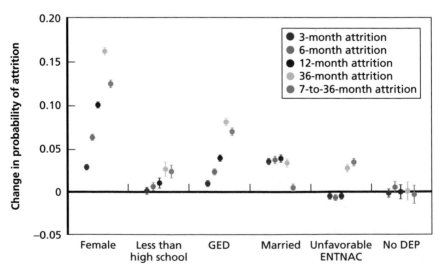

SOURCE: Author calculations from DMDC data merged with BLS data at the county level.
NOTE: Vertical bars represent 95-percent confidence intervals. N = 794,247.

Table B.2
Attrition Among Accessions in FYs 2003–2007 Versus FYs 2008–2013

Variable	Army		Air Force		Navy		Marine Corps	
	FYs 2003–2007	FYs 2008–2013	FYs 2003–2007	FYs 2008–2013	FYs 2003–2007	FYs 2008–2013	FYs 2003–2007	FYs 2008–2013
Number of accessions	77,179	794,247	37,209	320,542	43,920	394,987	32,140	349,229
Attrition rates (percentage)								
3-month attrition	6.9	4.9	4.4	5.1	6.1	6.3	7.1	5.1
6-month attrition	12.4	9.6	9.4	9.0	8.1	8.5	9.9	7.5
12-month attrition	17.7	14.7	13.1	12.1	12.4	11.7	13.8	10.2
36-month attrition	34.6	29.3	26.7	22.7	26.8	23.2	22.6	18.1

SOURCE: Author's calculation from DMDC data.

to those in Figure B.1. The most evident difference is that the magnitude of the marginal effect for women is 1 or 2 percentage points lower for the 12-month mark and beyond, although still statistically significant. In addition, the effect for those without a high school diploma is approximately 1 percentage point larger, and, unlike in Figure B.1, the three-month effect is statistically significant. Standard errors are larger than in Figure B.1 because the sample is smaller.

Figure B.2
Marginal Effects of Accession Characteristics on Attrition
for Army Enlistees in FYs 2008–2013

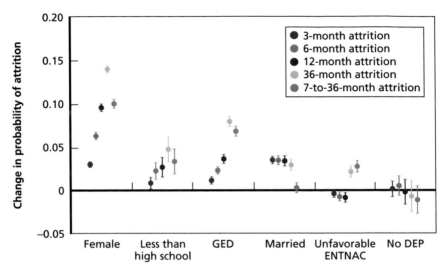

SOURCE: Author calculations from DMDC data merged with BLS data at the county level.
NOTE: Vertical bars represent 95-percent confidence intervals. N = 794,247.

References

Arkes, J., and J. M. Cunha, "Workplace Goals and Output Quality: Evidence from Time-Constrained Recruiting Goals in the US Navy," *Defence and Peace Economics*, Vol. 26, No. 5, 2014, pp. 491–515.

Arkes, J., and S. Mehay, "The Impact of the Unemployment Rate on Attrition of First-Term Enlistees," *Defence and Peace Economics*, Vol. 25, No. 2, 2013, pp. 125–138.

Asch, B. J., and P. Heaton, *An Analysis of the Incidence of Recruiter Irregularites*, Santa Monica, Calif.: RAND Corporation, TR-827-OSD, 2010. As of November 22, 2019:
https://www.rand.org/pubs/technical_reports/TR827.html

Asch, B. J., T. Miller, and G. Weinberger, *Can We Explain Gender Differences in Officer Career Progression?* Santa Monica, Calif.: RAND Corporation, RR-1288-OSD, 2016. As of December 3, 2019:
https://www.rand.org/pubs/research_reports/RR1288.html

Buddin, R. J., *Success of First-Term Soldiers: The Effects of Recruiting Practices and Recruit Characteristics*, Santa Monica, Calif.: RAND Corporation, MG-262-A, 2005. As of December 3, 2019:
https://www.rand.org/pubs/monographs/MG262.html

Carter, S. P., and A. Wozniak, "Making Big Changes: The Impact of Moves on Marriage Among U.S. Army Personnel," NBER Working Paper No. 24300, February 2018.

Cunha, J. M., J. Arkes, P. B. Lester, and Y.-C. Shen, "Employee Retention and Psychological Health: Evidence from Military Recruits," *Applied Economics Letters*, Vol. 22, No. 18, 2015, pp. 1505–1510.

Daniel, S., A. Neria, A. Moore, and E. Davis, "The Impact of Leadership Responses to Sexual Harassment and Gender Discrimination Reports on Emotional Distress and Retention Intentions in Military Members," *Journal of Trauma & Dissociation*, Vol. 20, No. 3, 2019, pp. 1–16.

Dertouzos, J. N., *The Cost-Effectiveness of Military Advertising: Evidence from 2002–2004*, Santa Monica, Calif.: RAND Corporation, DB-565-OSD, 2009. As of December 3, 2019:
https://www.rand.org/pubs/documented_briefings/DB565.html

Desrosiers, S., and E. Bradley, *Differences in Male and Female Predictors of Success in the Marine Corps: A Literature Review*, Arlington, Va.: Center for Naval Analyses, 2015.

Enns, J. H., *Cost Attrition: Army and Navy Results for FY2008*, Monterey, Calif.: Naval Postgraduate School, 2012.

Federal Reserve Bank of St. Louis, "Consumer Price Index for All Urban Consumers: All Items in U.S. City Average (CPIAUCNS)," FRED Economic Data, database, updated December 11, 2019. As of December 23, 2019:
https://fred.stlouisfed.org/series/CPIAUCNS

Germano, K., "Separate Is Not Equal in the Marine Corps," *New York Times*, March 31, 2018.

Gibson, J. L., and J. Hackenbracht, "An Event History Analysis of First-Term Soldier Attrition," *Military Psychology*, Vol. 26, No. 1, 2014, pp. 55–66.

Godlewski, R., and T. Kline, "A Model of Voluntary Turnover in Male Canadian Forces Recruits," *Military Psychology*, Vol. 24, No. 3, 2012, pp. 251–269.

Heckman, J. J., J. E. Humphries, and T. Kautz, eds., *The Myth of Achievement Tests: The GED and the Role of Character in American Life*, Chicago: University of Chicago Press, 2014.

Helmus, T. C., S. R. Zimmerman, M. N. Posard, J. L. Wheeler, C. Ogletree, Q. Stroud, and M. C. Harrell, *Life as a Private: A Study of the Motivations and Experiences of Junior Enlisted Personnel in the U.S. Army*, Santa Monica, Calif.: RAND Corporation, RR-2252-A, 2018. As of December 3, 2019:
https://www.rand.org/pubs/research_reports/RR2252.html

Hogan, P. F., and R. F. Seifert, "Marriage and the Military: Evidence That Those Who Serve Marry Earlier and Divorce Earlier," *Armed Forces & Society*, Vol. 36, No. 3, 2010, pp. 420–438.

Hoglin, P. J., and N. Barton, "First-Term Attrition of Military Personnel in the Australian Defence Force," *Armed Forces & Society*, Vol. 41, No. 1, 2013, pp. 43–68.

Hutchins, C. W., Jr., and R. S. Kennedy, *The Relationship Between Past History of Motion Sickness and Attrition from Flight Training*, Pensacola, Fla.: Naval School of Aviation Medicine, 1965.

Karaca-Mandic, P., N. Maestas, and D. Power, "Peer Groups and Employment Outcomes: Evidence Based on Conditional Random Assignment in the U.S. Army," unpublished draft, 2013.

Kiernan, M. D., *Identifying and Understanding Factors Associated with Failure to Complete Infantry Training Among British Army Recruits*, thesis, University of Nottingham, UK, 2011.

Knapik, J. J., B. H. Jones, K. Hauret, S. Darakjy, and E. Piskator, *A Review of the Literature on Attrition from the Military Services: Risk Factors for Attrition and Strategies to Reduce Attrition*, USACHPPM Report No. 12-HF-01Q9A-04, Aberdeen Proving Ground, Md.: U.S. Army Center for Health Promotion and Preventive Medicine, October 2004.

Knapp, D., B. R. Orvis, C. E. Maerzluft, and T. Tsai, *Resources Required to Meet the U.S. Army's Enlisted Recruiting Requirements Under Alternative Recruiting Goals, Conditions, and Eligibility Policies*, Santa Monica, Calif.: RAND Corporation, RR-2364-A, 2018. As of December 3, 2019:
https://www.rand.org/pubs/research_reports/RR2364.html

Laurence, J. H., "The Military Performance of GED Holders," in J. J. Heckman, J. E. Humphries, and T. Kautz, eds., *The Myth of Achievement Tests: The GED and the Role of Character in American Life*, Chicago: University of Chicago Press, 2014, pp. 268–292.

Lucas, J. W., Y. Whitestone, D. R. Segal, and M. W. Segal, *The Role of Social Support in First-Term Sailors' Attrition from Recruit Training*, Millington, Tenn.: Navy Personnel Research Studies and Technology Division Bureau of Naval Personnel, 2008.

Lundquist, J. H., D. Pager, and E. Strader, "Does a Criminal Past Predict Worker Performance? Evidence from One of America's Largest Employers," *Social Forces*, Vol. 96, No. 3, 2018, pp. 1039–1068.

Lundquist, J. H., and Z. Xu, "Reinstitutionalizing Families: Life Course Policy and Marriage in the Military," *Journal of Marriage and Family*, Vol. 76, No. 5, 2014, pp. 1063–1081.

Malone, L., "Hiring from High-Risk Populations: Lessons from the U.S. Military," *Contemporary Economic Policy*, Vol. 32, No. 1, 2014, pp. 133–143.

Malone, L., and N. Carey, *Waivered Recruits: An Evaluation of Their Performance and Attrition Risk*, Arlington, Va.: Center for Naval Analyses, 2011.

Morral, A. R., K. L. Gore, and T. L. Schell, eds., *Sexual Assault and Sexual Harassment in the U.S. Military: Volume 2. Estimates for Department of Defense Service Members from the 2014 RAND Military Workplace Study*, Santa Monica, Calif.: RAND Corporation, RR-870/2-1-OSD, 2015. As of December 3, 2019:
https://www.rand.org/pubs/research_reports/RR870z2-1.html

Orvis, B. R., C. E. Maerzluft, S.-B. Kim, M. G. Shanley, and H. Krull, *Prospective Outcome Assessment for Alternative Recruit Selection Policies*, Santa Monica, Calif.: RAND Corporation, RR-2267-A, 2018. As of December 3, 2019:
https://www.rand.org/pubs/research_reports/RR2267.html

Philipps, D., and T. Gibbons-Neff, "Marines to Integrate Female and Male Training Battalions for First Time," *New York Times*, January 4, 2019.

Plag, J. A., and J. M. Goffman, "The Prediction of Four-Year Military Effectiveness in Characteristics of Naval Recruits," *Military Medicine*, Vol. 131, No. 8, 1966, pp. 729–735.

Plag, J. A., and L. E. Hardacre, *The Validity of Age, Education, and GCT Score as Predictors of Two-Year Attrition Among Naval Enlistees*, San Diego, Calif.: Navy Medical Neuropsychiatric Research Unit, 1964.

Pollack, L. M., C. B. Boyer, K. Betsinger, and M.-A. Shafer, "Predictors of One-Year Attrition in Female Marine Corps Recruits," *Military Medicine*, Vol. 174, No. 8, 2009, pp. 382–391.

Reis, J. P., D. W. Trone, C. A. Macera, and M. J. Rauh, "Factors Associated with Discharge During Marine Corps Basic Training," *Military Medicine*, Vol. 172, No. 9, 2007, pp. 936–941.

Schehl, M. L., "Marine 1-Star Defends Gender Segregation at Boot Camp," *Marine Corps Times*, May 17, 2016.

Strickland, W. J., ed., *A Longitudinal Examination of First Term Attrition and Reenlistment Among FY1999 Enlisted Accessions*, Arlington, Va.: U.S. Army Research Institute for the Behavioral and Social Sciences, Technical Report No. 1172, November 2005.

U.S. Department of Defense Instruction 1304.23, *Acquisition and Use of Criminal History Record Information for Military Recruiting Purposes*, Washington, D.C., October 7, 2005.

White, M. R., C. J. Phillips, K. J. Vyas, and L. Bauer, "Demographic and Psychosocial Predictors of Early Attrition for Drug Use in the U.S. Marines," *Military Medicine*, Vol. 181, Nos. 11–12, 2016, pp. e1540–e1545.

Wolfe, J., K. Turner, M. Caulfield, T. L. Newton, K. Melia, J. Martin, and J. Goldstein, "Gender and Trauma as Predictors of Military Attrition: A Study of Marine Corps Recruits," *Military Medicine*, Vol. 170, No. 12, 2005, pp. 1037–1043.